CHIEVELEY

Remembered

BILL MARTIN

Best wishes

Bill M

TRAFFORD
PUBLISHING™

Note for Librarians: a cataloguing record for this book that includes Dewey Decimal
Classification and US Library of Congress numbers is available from the Library and Archives
of Canada. The complete cataloguing record can be obtained from their online database at:
www.collectionscanada.ca/amicus/index-e.html
ISBN 1-4251-0246-8
Printed in Victoria, BC, Canada

Printed on paper with minimum 30% recycled fibre.
Trafford's print shop runs on "green energy" from solar, wind and other environmentally-friendly power sources.

TRAFFORD
PUBLISHING

Offices in Canada, USA, Ireland and UK
This book was published *on-demand* in cooperation with Trafford Publishing. On-demand
publishing is a unique process and service of making a book available for retail sale to the
public taking advantage of on-demand manufacturing and Internet marketing. On-demand
publishing includes promotions, retail sales, manufacturing, order fulfilment, accounting and
collecting royalties on behalf of the author.

Book sales for North America and international:
Trafford Publishing, 6E–2333 Government St.,
Victoria, BC v8t 4p4 CANADA
phone 250 383 6864 (toll-free 1 888 232 4444)
fax 250 383 6804; email to orders@trafford.com
Book sales in Europe:
Trafford Publishing (uk) Ltd., Enterprise House, Wistaston Road Business Centre,
Wistaston Road, Crewe, Cheshire cw2 7rp UNITED KINGDOM
phone 01270 251 396 (local rate 0845 230 9601)
facsimile 01270 254 983; orders.uk@trafford.com
Order online at:
trafford.com/06-2003

10 9 8 7 6 5 4 3 2

INTRODUCTION

THIS BOOK IS a record of my memories of changes and incidents which have taken place in Chieveley during my lifetime.

Seventy years or so of history can never be covered in just a few pages of print, but it is my sincere wish that these somewhat rambling reminiscences of a 'Chieveley Old Boy' may give the reader a brief insight into the past way of life and the vast changes that have taken place.

There are a few people who have lived in the village longer than myself and whose memories are clearer than my own. My friend Vera Pocock has also spent many years in making notes such as these and she has also amassed a wonderful collection of old photographs. Most of all, my sincere thanks go to my dear wife Gillian. The whole thing was her idea and she has been responsible for promoting, typing and editing this work and without her enthusiasm none of these memories would have been set down in print.

The initial idea was to record a few memories and anecdotes to hand on to my grandchildren in the hope that they might be interested in the history of the village. However the whole thing seems to have escalated somewhat and may also be of interest to those who now live in the village.

W.F.J.M.2006

CHAPTER ONE

THE NAME CHIEVELEY is thought to have been derived from a translation referred to in "The History of Chieveley" by the Revd. B.H.Bravery Attlee written in 1919, who was at that time Vicar of the parish. The name "field of chives" is believed to refer to the field of allium which until recent times grew in profusion at the edges of the field to the rear of Coombe House (formerly the Vicarage). The chives would have have originated from meals eaten by Roman soldiers who were reputed to have camped there.

The brother of the Chieveley Vicar was Clement Attlee, who was Prime Minister of this country from 1945 to 1951, a period which saw the introduction of the National Health Service and independence granted to India and Burma.

St. Mary's Church is the oldest building in the village,. Parts of the church dating back to Norman times. A list of past incumbents hangs on the south wall inside the main door.

After World War I the church yard was in a very dilapidated state and a group of recently returned soldiers were employed in restoring it to the excellent state in which we see it today. Many headstones were repositioned, not necessarily in their original situations, having fallen down over the years. Paths were laid and trees were planted.

Also in the churchyard stood a wooden building which was home to the mower and other tools but its main function was to house the village bier. This was in frequent use before the days of the motorised hearse. Its whereabouts today is unknown but it was probably disposed of when the present more modern shed was erected. The door of the old shed was never locked and allowed persons tending graves to have access to the various tools etc. Sadly today's building has taken on a more 'Fort Knox' appearance, the inside being lined with steel mesh and the mowing machines having to be locked and chained to the floor to prevent their being stolen.

During the time that Brian Goodrich was Vicar, the Church yard had become full and so an additional area was consecrated to the south of the old one. Since this time, the new area has become more than half filled. Quite a sobering experience it is to walk through this place and realise that one knew most of the people buried there. With cremations being more popular these days, the pressure for burial space should be lessened and a special area is set aside for the interment of ashes..

Many of the graves of my ancestors on my Mother's side are marked by headstones in Chieveley Churchyard. These include members of several families whose names are mentioned in the Parish Register; Hiscock, Barrett and Leach. From these families came Julia Anne Barrett and Frederick Leach, my Grandparents. They lived in a cottage in Horsemoor, where my mother was born, the third of four children, one girl and three boys, and christened Gladys Kathleen Nellie, but was always known as Kate. She attended Chieveley School and on leaving was employed by Shepherd's in a clerical capacity.

My father's parents lived in Lewisham where he was born in 1890. His father, William, a retired soldier, came from Ireland and died three years after my father was born. My father then moved, with his Welsh mother, and two older brothers to Tilbury. His mother died when he was twelve years old. His two brothers emigrated to Canada and he was brought up by an older half-sister at Herne Bay. At seventeen by adding a year to his age, he joined the army at the beginning of the first World War.

He served with the Hampshire Regiment on the Somme and at

Ypres and was duly promoted to the rank of Sergeant. He was also a member of the army boxing team. This was followed by a tour of duty in Turkey and in 1919 he served in Northern Ireland. On leaving the army he found work dismantling an engineering plant at Curridge Brick Works. During the mid 1920's he was employed by the Broad family at Priors Court Farm. At this time his prowess as a boxer continued and he was a founder member of a boxing club which met regularly in one of the farm buildings.

During his army careeer he excelled as an athlete, mainly on sprint and middle distance running, for which he was awarded several gold medals and other trophies. He was also an accomplished footballer, and played for his Regiment. The team reached the final of the Army Cup Final in 1920 and he received his runner's up medal from their Majesties King George V and Queen Mary. A prized family possession is a photograph of this unique occasion. In later years, he continued to play football for Chieveley and was also a regular member of the Cricket Club. Whilst working in the Chieveley area, he met my mother and they were married by the Reverend H. Bravery Attlee on August 4th 1928, the reception being held in the Memorial Hall opposite the School. They began their married life in a cottage in Curridge. The great depression was just beginning and together with many others, my father found himself out of work and consequently spent some time in the aforementioned reorganizing of Chieveley Church Yard.

Soon after this he found employment as a gardener for Mr. Francis T. Dallin at Coombe House. A cottage went with the job and they moved in during the early part of 1929. In August the following year in the presence of the District Nurse and Doctor Risien, armed with forceps, I made my complaining entry into this world.

CHAPTER TWO

FOR MANY YEARS Bob Weaver was organist at St. Mary's. A strong choir of men and boys sang under his direction, and at the age eight I joined the choir. In the Reverend Hazel's time, after the choir had sung carols outside the Red Lion pub, Mr. Thomas, the Landlord who must have been moved by the Christmas spirit, came to the door carrying a tray of glasses of ginger wine. These of course had to be consumed outside, as no persons under the age of 18 was allowed in the premises. We felt very grown up especially as the going rate for ginger wine was at that time four pence a glass (just under 2 new pence). The Reverend Hazel also held lantern slide shows in the Vicarage barn, mostly depicting his life and times in Africa. These were always very popular with the younger element, he also had a wonderful collection of African war clubs, shields and assegais. We were never allowed to handle them which was probably a very wise decision on his part.

A few years ago the Reverend Hazel's son John and his wife returned to St. Mary's church to renew their wedding vows on the occasion of their Diamond Anniversary. They had been married by John's father by special licence prior to his being posted overseas in the early part of the 1940's. It was also a pleasant memory for me as

I was also a member of the choir at the original service.

Some years later, the Reverend Goodrich also incorporated lantern slide shows during Evensong in the Church. His commentaries were particularly interesting especially when relating to his time spent as a Commissioner of Police in Singapore.

Violet Webber spent her early days in Boxford and moved to Chieveley after marrying Leon who had been her music teacher. After so many years as Church organist we can only say what a remarkable job he did in teaching her. Half a century on and after teaching at the local school for most of that time, she left her house in the High Street and moved into Newbury. This does not prevent her from playing at St. Mary's, accompanying the Chieveley Singers when they perform to various charity groups and organisations, and playing for the annual Carols for Everyone in the Village Hall in the winter time. When Vi took over as Church Organist, ladies and young girls joined the choir, which continued to prosper under her direction. During her time, the organ was moved into the body of the church and is now operated by an electrically driven fan. This is an improvement on the days when it took two boys pumping furiously to provide enough power for Bob Weaver to play the pop tunes of the 1930's and 40's, this of course was after the Revd. Hazel had gone home.

I can remember the new carved oak screen at the West end being dedicated in 1935/6 and I think the font was moved to its existing position at the same time.

Chieveley had a very nice ring of six quite heavy bells and a new steel bell frame was installed in 1980 to replace the old original oak timber frame which had been in use for several hundred years. Two extra bells were hung some years later, making a ring of eight. The two new bells were added during the incumbency of Colin Scott-Dempster, whose name appears on one of the bells. A team of dedicated ringers are there for most services under the captaincy of Mr. Rod Brown, following in the footsteps of Mr. Frank Tuffley, who was captain for many years. I rang at Chieveley for some twenty years together with some of the famous local ringers of the time. Gilbert Townsend (Chieveley) Mark Rosier (Peasemore) Reg Rex (Thatcham) Reg Crook (Yattendon) and Frank Tuffley (Chieveley) were all prominent ringers and their names appear in the Honours Boards in the towers of the most of the churches in the locality where peals in various methods have been rung often to celebrate some special event. These stalwarts would cycle for many miles sometimes in the dark and wet to attend the practice nights and to help beginners master the art of change-ringing.

Over the years many improvements have been made to the Church. In the Reverend Scott-Dempster's time, some of the pews were removed at the rear of the Church to allow for a communal area and for coffee to be served after some of the services. In 1964 the heating was improved by the installation of an oil fired boiler, this work carried out by the writer, for the princely sum of £468. 10 shillings, to include the boiler, tank and electrical work..

Although the temperatures in the Church improved, little has been done to improve the comfort of the seating in St. Mary's or indeed in any of our other local churches.

I recall visiting Beedon Church for the marriage of my cousin, David Leach, on a very cold day in the mid 1950's. We had reached that part of the service when the Registers had to be signed and the vicar appealed to the congregation, sitting huddled in their seats, for the loan of a fountain pen. The old style pen with the nib could not be used as the contents of the ink bottle were frozen solid. This was before the advent of ball-point pens, but for some years after their introduction they could not be used to sign any form of legal document due to the fact that the ink was liable to fade.

In St. Mary's Church a loop system was also installed to help the hard of hearing which was further improved in 2004..

The "Upper Rooms" and toilet facilities were added in the 1980's, the cost of this work being financed from the sale of the Old Infant School in the High Street.. To the right of the West door is an ordnance survey mark which shows this part of the County to be 600 ft above sea level.

The details of St. Marys Church, are well documented in the Reverend Attlee's book and a history of most of the happenings which took place up to the nineteen twenties. Another booklet giving details of our Church has been compiled by June Butcher. This has been recently updated and copies are obtainable from the Church.

CHAPTER THREE

Most of the properties in Chieveley are of brick and tile construction, although many of the older houses would originally have had thatched roofs. The bricks used would have been produced locally from one or other of the three brick kilns in the vicinity. The first of these kilns was at Beedon on the west side of the old A34 road at the top of the hill. The second yard was at Curridge to the west of the New Inn. In its heyday, the output of bricks other than those used for local building were transported for distribution to Newbury Railway Station by horse and cart. This brickworks had almost ceased trading before the coming of the railway to Hermitage. After its closure as a brick works it became an industrial estate owned by Mr. Ron Bates eventually being developed for housing in the late 1980's.

From the mid-1940's onward the majority of the bricks used by the construction industry were made by the London Brick Company and transported all over the country by their fleet of red painted lorries. The many millions of bricks produced came from their works in the Bletchley area of Buckinghamshire and the skyline of that huge area of clay ground was filled with chimney stacks from the numerous kilns. All these bricks were loaded on and off by hand, and straw placed between the layers of facing bricks to prevent damage during transportation. One has to experience off-loading many thousands of bricks in all sorts of weather, to fully appreciate the amount of effort involved. This monopoly continued for some fifty years but since that time, production is now carried out in various other areas, bricks being transported on pre-packed pallets and the loading and off-loading undertaken mechanically, with all the various health and safety procedures attendant.

With the coming of metrication the common brick became slightly larger. Prior to this time it was always possible to check the height of a building quite accurately, as laid, bricks measured four courses to the foot vertically.

The third and by far the largest local brick and tile works was Pinewood, at Hermitage. This had a continuous kiln as well as several beehive pattern kilns which produced roofing tiles. Some of the bricks produced here were of the very highest quality and in great demand. This kiln continued to operate until the end of the second World War and produced bricks and tiles in great numbers, having its own railway siding and a small station known as Pinewood Halt, off the Didcot to Winchester railway line. This line had been increased from single to double track during the war to cope with an ever increasing number of troop trains and those carrying war materials but was closed in the early 1960's as part of the Beeching plan.

In the village few of the traditional timber frame structures remain and those that do are mostly converted farm buildings. Thatch used for roofing was mainly wheat straw and threshed in a particular manner to render it suitable for the job. The feeder or man whose job it was to feed the sheaves into the drum of the threshing machine would normally allow the whole sheaf to enter the drum. In order to keep the stalks of the wheat straw as long and straight as possible, the sheaves would be held into the drum so that only the ears containing the corn were removed. The straw would then be tied into bundles and carefully stored until required by the thatcher. There are few buildings roofed with slate, a material which would have come from Wales. Most of the dwellings erected during the first half of the twentieth century would have been built by a local building firm, usually a family business, who would have employed local tradesmen, unlike today where specialist sub-contractors follow each other as the work progresses.

CHAPTER FOUR

CHURCH LANE GOES from the High Street to the Church and also serves the main entrance to the Manor. At the High Street end the first house on the left is called "Rosedale" and was for many years the home of Philip and Olive Cockeril. He had been a prisoner of war in Japanese hands and moved to the village immediately after the end of the war. He was a leading authority on postage stamps and ran a business from the house. He was also for many years Clerk to the Parish Council and keen member of the Chieveley Tennis Club. At the end of "Rosedale" garden is the rear entrance to Shepherd's bakery.

The cottage on the left near the Church gate has been home to members of several well known village families, in particular Bert Bune who was employed at the Manor and Jack Pike who was a baker for Shepherds for many years having moved there from Rookery Cottage in Manor Lane.

Opposite stands the new Vicarage, the first occupants of this building being the Reverend Scott-Dempster and his family, who moved there from the old Vicarage,and he remained there until August 2003 when on his retirement, after twenty nine years in the Parish, he and his family moved to Scotland.

Our new Vicar, the Reverend John Toogood, whose official title is Priest in Charge, took over St. Mary's Church together with St. James the Less Winterbourne and St. Bartholome's at Oare in October 2003. He has settled in extremely well and is much liked by all the parishioners. It is hoped that he and his wife Phillipa and young daughter Charlotte have a long and happy time in our village.

Manor Lodge is the only other house in Church Lane. This house also has been home to many Chieveley families. Geoffrey Pocock, gardener at the Manor lived there for a long time with his wife and family Vera and Michael. Jack Winter also gardener at the Manor after Mr.Pocock, lived there for many years to be followed by Pat Pocock and his wife Grace who were also employed at the Manor until their retirement. This house has now undergone a major extension..

Standing at the end of Church Lane, the first house on the Left hand side is "The Maypole", at one time home to Commodore Gibbons (Ret'd) of the Cunard White Star Shipping Line. On one occasion, when I was repairing a leak in the water main under the wall, at the corner of Church Lane, Commodore Gibbons, watching operations, strutted backwards and forwards, hands behind his back and looking extremely concerned., said "I once had the "Mauritania" aground Mr. Martin, but I wasn't half as worried about that as I am now!"

The work being carried out involved excavating adjacent to the main stop-cock in the road and trenching under the boundary wall to a point some six feet across the lawn, all to a depth of two feet, then replacing the faulty section of water main, backfilling the trench, making good the surface of the road and re-laying the garden turf. This work was undertaken on September 23rd and 24th 1957. Labour charges (eleven hours) £3 17 shillings, materials £1. 9s 4d making a grand total of £5 6s 11d. thank goodness there was no v.a.t. to add.

CHAPTER FIVE

OPPOSITE THE "MAYPOLE" is a now very little-used bus shelter but one which saw much service when the village was served by buses between Newbury and Oxford,. when double-decker buses left the "Church Corner" at ten minutes to each hour in each direction. This resulted in many traffic problems outside Shepherd's shop, which not only had delivery vehicles and customers parking in the narrow part of the High Street, but also had two petrol pumps providing fuel for motorists.

Behind the wall at the rear of the bus stop, stands the Old Vicarage, built in the early 1720's, a lovely building which was home to the parish vicars until the new vicarage was erected in about 1979. The Reverend Colin Scott Dempster and family then moved from this house and to become the first tenants of the New Vicarage in Church Lane.

In my lifetime, there have been six vicars who lived in the Old Vicarage. In the large garden were stables, garages and a larger building known as the Vicarage barn (now converted to a dwelling). This was the venue for many events and most of the village people learned to dance there to the music of "The Downend Band" (Mrs. V. Bune, piano, son Gordon on piano accordion and Eric Cox on drums. The entrance fee was 6d. Socials and whist drives were regular events and a Chieveley Table Tennis Club was formed in the 1960's, and its members played in the Newbury Table Tennis League for several seasons.

The format of the Socials were often varied, but adults as well as children joined in the games; musical chairs, and bean-bags, which were cotton bags containing haricot beans, were tossed at a vertical board which had holes indicating the various scores. Bagatelle was also played and Beetle Drives were popular, often followed by dancing. Most of these past-times may be considered to be 'old hat' today but before the advent of television there was little else to do. People talked to each other much more than they do now, both in the home and outside. They also had little opportunity to travel as buses were few and far between and not many people owned a car, and those who did were loath to travel any distance because of strict fuel rationing applied during the war years. Another handicap at this time were the stringent blackout regulations. It was illegal to show any form of light and black curtains would be drawn across windows and doors before any internal light could be turned on. This made things quite cosy during the winter but temperatures could become very uncomfortable in the warmer weather. Visors were fitted to the headlamps of motor vehicles which allowed a very restricted amount of light to show through. This resulted in reduced speeds but an increase in minor accidents.

During war time another difficulty confronting the traveller was the fact that all signposts and Railway station names had been removed as a safety measure to confuse possible enemy agents. The genuine traveller could seldom get help as to where he was or how to get to his destination, for people were warned by large posters and wireless programmes not to give any information to a stranger. Such slogans as "Careless Talk Costs Lives" and "Walls Have Ears" and "Be like Dad Keep Mum", were prominently displayed.

The staff wing of the Old Vicarage has also been turned into a separate dwelling and another large new house has been erected on the site of what used to be the Vicarage chicken run, located between the Barn and Coombe House. The Barn and adjoining stables and garage buildings have also been converted into homes. Several lorry loads of sand were tipped outside the stables at the beginning of the war and some of the older school boys, including myself aged ten, were recruited to fill many hundreds of sand bags. However I cannot recall seeing any of them being used in the village.

Opposite stands The Cottage and Dial Cottage. The Cottage, formerly the home of Maurice Taylor and family was modernised by Reg and June Goodchild who have lived there since 1956. Dial Cottage next door, is so called because of sun dial on the front elevation. With more and more people becoming owners of motor vehicles the entrances to many properties were altered to accommodate this new means of transport. Originally the only entrance to the these two properties was by means of a small wicket gate set in the middle of the front wall. This usually hung open allowing entrance to the cottages by way of a gravel path which wound its way through the cottage garden,.the main feature being a large Victoria plum tree which each year supplied an abundance of fruit. This in turn led to many of its branches being propped up with an assortment of 'aids' such as baulks of timber, old cast iron rainwater pipes and the like, to prevent the crop bringing the overloaded branches down. This was not a pretty sight but offset by the mouthwatering thought of plum pies and home made jam. Also in the garden was a deep well with a wooden structure housing the winding gear. Long ago this would have served several adjoining properties as well as the two cottages.

The next house had several owners, including Mr. and Mrs. Cyril Fry, Mrs. Ruth Harper, Mr. and Mrs. Dawbarn, Mrs. Ann Rayner.. Originally known as The Niche it was renamed Marymead in Mrs. Harper's time. The large garden at the rear of the property and the site now occupied by the new Vicarage was formerly a paddock which contained several large elm trees, another popular nesting place for rooks. This paddock was known as the Rookery.

Nubian House, later called "The Old Bakehouse" halfway along the West side of the High street, was a prosperous shop selling groceries, owned by the Prismall family and until the war was also a bakers. Prismall's was once the largest shop in the village and served many adjoining villages, deliveries being made by horse-drawn vehicles and with the coming of the motor they ran at least three vans. The shop also had a slaughter house and the majority of the meat sold was killed on the premises, all of which would have been raised by local farmers. The Prismall family lived here initially but later the family home was "The Limes" while Bob Snell, who was the Manager lived with his family at The Maypole. When Prismall's sold up, he opened a grocery business in Compton.

Ern 'Baker' Leach, my Grandfather's brother was baker for Prismalls who at this time still used wood-fired ovens. Baffins or bundles of wood usually hazel, were placed in the brick oven and lighted. When they had burnt out, the ashed were raked from the oven and the dough placed in the hot brick-lined oven to bake. One winter's day after a heavy snow fall I was playing with John Phillips in Prismall's yard and we thought it might be a good idea to fill the bread oven with snow. This was duly undertaken causing poor old Ern a lot of extra work. Being the wonderfully kind man that he was, he laughed it off, saying, "Boys will be boys". We would have been about ten years old at the time.

Prismalls old shop was taken over and fully modernized in the early part of the war by Mr. Norris. However a disastrous fire gutted the whole place. After re-building, it was reopened and was later sold to Mr. Willis and his wife and two daughters, he having recently left the Royal Air Force. Mr. Willis ran the grocer's shop and sold it on as a going concern to Mr. and Mrs. Chase in the early 60's. Mr. Chase was a builder and turned the top floors into flats. The adjoining Stables, old Bake house, slaughter house and stores were demolished to make way for the existing Maisonette.The main house has since been turned back to a single dwelling.

Next to The Maisonette, is The Chalet, so called because of its overhanging eaves and was from my earliest recollection occupied by Bill Leach and his wife Kitty (my aunt and uncle). He was the village bootmaker and repairer and operated from a workshop on the first floor of the building in Pig Lane (now referred to as Manor Lane). This house is now called The Whitehouse

During the early years of the war, my uncle, Jack Leach and his wife Kath and sons David and Derek, lived at the Chalet with Uncle Bill and Aunty Kit. As young boys we always seemed to be in some sort of trouble. One day, David stuck a garden fork into his foot by accident, the point of which came out through the sole of his shoe.

This was sorted out by Nurse Taylor. Another time we had been to Prismall's shop next door and returned with several damaged tins of floor polish, which had been thrown away. This we spread on to Uncle Bill's lawn to make a slide. His comments are not suitable for publication. We then put the empty polish tins through Aunty Kit's mangle which stood just inside the back door. This machine had wooden rollers and when used to flatten metal polish tins, rendered it almost useless for its intended purpose. I forget the 'rewards' we collected for this venture.

As schoolboys we would often call in to see Uncle Bill in his upstairs workshop in Manor Lane, busily repairing boots and shoes. It was also not unknown for us to pocket a handful of boot studs, steel studs similar to large drawing pins which were driven into the soles of leather boots to prolong their wear. These ' borrowed' studs would be carefully placed in a line across the road. We would then lie in wait to see how many were picked up the wheels of any passing vehicle. They were not long enough to puncture a car or bus tyre but one day we caught Mr. Frank 'Crapper' Holliday on his postman's bicycle. He in turn caught us, bringing that form of sport to rather an abrupt end.

CHAPTER SIX

MANOR LANE, FOOTPATH number 10, runs from The High Street in a westerly direction to the rear entrance of the Manor and then continues as a footpath to Grove road towards the Ford and Hazelhanger.Near the back entrance to the Manor another path FP 10/38 travels northward and joins Gidley lane Bridleway 11. Where it crosses Old street, it is known as the 'burial path' this name being derived from the fact that before the building of the Church in Leckhampstead, the dead from the Leckhampstead area were carried along this path to Chieveley for burial, either by means of a bier or perhaps using a horse drawn vehicle if the path was of sufficient width in those days. If these methods were not practicable then the only other way would have been on the shoulders of the bearers, a distance of some three or more miles.

From the High Street to the rear entrance to the Manor, Pig Lane was only some twelve feet in width (4 metres) but was increased to its existing width with the building of Corner House and the properties on the north side in 1958.

The cottage adjoining the workshop on the south side is known as Rookery Cottage, at one time the home of Jack Pike and one of the few cottages in the village to retain a brick built outside privy in the garden (not currently in use). This cottage had a garden of insufficient size to allow the contents of the privy bucket to be disposed of on site. Therefore the task was taken care of by a weekly visit from the 'Honey Wagon' which fortunately called early morning.

Further along the lane in approximately the position of Harry Argent's driveway entrance stood an old thatched cottage which was home to Harold Bosley and his family before they moved to Southfields. This cottage was demolished and two bungalows built on the site by the writer. The last bungalow on the North side of the lane, known as "Wishanger" was built by Jack Acton who for some years was Clerk to the Parish Council. This bungalow has since had another storey added.

On the other side of the lane is a pair of cottages once occupied by Mrs. Smith and her son George and in the adjoining cottage lived Mr. And Mrs.George Willoughby. These were converted to a single dwelling in the 1950's and then occupied by Mr. Peter Weaver and his wife. During the ensuing years the property has since changed hands several times.

Next stands a bungalow named "Crossways" built by Geoffrey Pocock after his retirement from the Manor. This is now owned by daughter Vera and son Michael. Vera has spent many years compiling a pictorial history of the village and written a contribution to "The History of Chieveley 2000AD" in collaboration with her cousin Victor Pocock, this work gives a very detailed description of the village over many generations.

Michael Pocock has inherited his father's gardening skills and has developed them to such a degree as to become a top showman and judge, always ready to answer any questions on horticulture and much sought after as a lecturer at local horticultural and gardening club meetings. He is perhaps fortunate to be able to do this since when he was a schoolboy he had an argument with a Newbury & District bus, finishing on the losing side, by having the bus run over his leg. This no doubt prevented him from representing England at football but otherwise led to no long term disability.

The only remaining property in the lane is Little Manor built in the 1960's and occupied since that time by a very keen horticulturalist who has a very nice garden on what was once part of the farmyard of the Manor.

Also at the rear of the Manor was an orchard and walled kitchen garden. The orchard was removed to allow the building of a tennis court and the walled garden now encloses a swimming pool. During the time Mr. and Mrs. Simon Courtauld were at the Manor, a relation (an uncle I believe) brought a team of archaealogical students who excavated several trenches in the orchard. This dig coincided with a job the writer was carrying out in front of the Manor to form the existing water garden. Several lorry loads of soil were brought to the site by the contractors who were at that time widening the School road. In one such load was a large thigh bone of a horse or cow. This was of some considerable age, so for a lark it was carefully placed in the bottom of one of the archaealogical trenches and covered with soil. The following week when the bone was duly discovered it was despatched to London for carbon dating amidst great excitement by the students. I never did find out the results and as Jack Winter and myself were the only two who knew of the hoax an enquiry would have probably brought disastrous consequences.

CHAPTER SEVEN

OPPOSITE MANOR LANE is Coombe House. This lovely old house has a large garden to the rear and adjoins land previously known as Vicarage Park. The view of the parkland from the house is bounded by a ha-ha. This is also the site of the alliums (chives) growing, as referred to in the earlier notes. The age of this house is unknown but it was certainly used as "The Rectory" until 1720, when the then Vicar built a new and much grander Vicarage on adjoining land immediately to the South, and so the house became known as Coombe House. It was the first house in the Village to have its own water supply pumped mechanically. This was first powered by a Lister petrol engine and later by an electrically operated motor. This system remained in use until the advent of the mains water supply to the Village in the mid-1930's. At the time of writing, Coombe House is for sale and offers in the region of £900,000 are invited. Some difference from fifty years ago when the house together with the gardener's cottage was bought for under £15,000.

The house was owned by Mr. F..T.Dallin who was for many years a Churchwarden and had been a Tax collector in Egypt. This no doubt accounted for the fabulous array of carpets, and artefacts which filled the place. His wife was an accomplished musician who played

the violin with several local orchestras and many famous names in
the music world visited the house. After Mr. Dallin's death, his wife
lived for many years at New Farm House.

I well remember some of the staff who were at Coombe House
during my school days, Mr and Mrs Arthur and Susan Bendle and
Mr and Mrs Sturgess. Mr. Sturgess was an accomplished pianist
and was allowed to play the grand piano in the Drawing Room. He
also played the piano in the Downend Band and was instrumental
in kitting out the players in gold coloured shirts. These splendid
garments were made by my Grandmother. Just before the war,
following the Sturgesses came two Swiss girls by the name of Rose
and Emme. Two very striking looking girls and much sort after by
the local Romeos. These lads however, were soon called away for
active service. Rose returned to Switzerland to be married and was
replaced by another girl named Erna. She and Emme stayed on for
several years and were only able to return to their native country
after the liberation of France.

Aunty Kit who lived opposite at the Chalet, occasionally worked
for the Dallins as a relief cook and I recall her often sending me
some fried potato chips when my Father went each evening to
stoke the central heating boiler. Chips were a rare delicacy during
food rationing , cooking fats being in short supply and of course
before the introduction of cooking oil. These chips would have been
cooked in lard and I cannot ever remember having chips cooked at
home. Many years later a favourite stop was Somerscales Fish and
Chip Restaurant in London Road Newbury. This establishment was
renowned for its food and to my knowledge the only shop of its kind
with its own restaurant.

Next to Coombe House stand Walnut Tree Cottages the larger of
these being for many years the home of Miss Woolaston and Miss
Carmichael, the smaller cottage being occupied by Nurse Martin.

On Miss Carmichael's death in 1959 Miss Woolaston moved into
the smaller dwelling, when Nurse Martin moved to Radnall's Farm
cottage. At this time John Griffin the Architect, and his family moved
into the larger of the two Walnut Tree Cottages. There was a very
attractive garden attached to these cottages and my father helped to
keep these in good order for Miss Woolaston, always affectionally

known as 'Old Woolly'.

On the opposite side of the road we have the aptly named Corner House built by the writer, who was not responsible for the front porch and extension which was added later by others. This site was originally occupied by a timber Tudor style house or Rectory with adjoining thatched barn. Also on this site was an extremely deep well, with mechanical winding gear which allowed water to be drawn by the use of two buckets, one travelling in either direction. This well would have served the surrounding comunity as well as the adjoining Rectory Farm.

Many smaller wells were used for drinking water and most cottages had underground rainwater tanks to store water for washing and laundry purpose. This water would have been raised from the tanks by means of semi-rotary hand pumps or by bucket and rope. Laundry was done in coppers fired by wood and usually situated in an outbuilding or wash house. At the rear of the old Rectory site stood the remains of a large row of brick built 'privies'. One was reputed to have housed a 'four-holer' to accommodate a complete family at one sitting. A pencil sketch of the Rectory has been attributed to Reverend Attlee and gives a good impression of what the Old Rectory may have looked like. The barn and adjoining cottage, always known as 'The Crooked House' were demolished at the time the Corner House was built by the writer who lived there for some thirty years, the old Rectory already having been demolished many years prior to this.

After the building of "The Corner House" the site was developed both in Manor Lane and the High Street. The site at the Northern end of the of the area became the first purpose built Doctor's Surgery in the village .Before this time when Dr. John Richards first moved to the village, he ran his surgery from East Lane. Later he was joined by Dr. Jack Nickson and Dr. David Arnold. The new surgery was built in the 1960's to serve what has become quite a large practice due partly to the retirement of the doctors in Ilsley and Brightwalton. The new building soon proved to be too small and was more than doubled in size. Even this extension was unable to cope and another new surgery was built in East Lane where formerly the Hare & Hounds pub stood. Latterly, the new surgery has also been increased in size and now has a team of some six doctors, operating as The

Downland Practice. There is also a Handybus service which is run for the benefit of patients and shoppers living in outlying districts.

CHAPTER EIGHT

In the High Street on the west side , some fifty yards North of Coombe House, stood Rectory Farm consisting of a large thatched barn, cart sheds (part still remaining) stables (which were destroyed by fire) and a brick built pig unit. There were also a pair of Thatched cottages, one of which housed the Carter. Quite an important man on a farm which used six or seven horses. Tractors came into general farm use in the late 1930's and the use of the horse finally ended some twenty years later.

Opposite the farm on the site of Dr. Arnold's former house, stood a timber building where Mr. Craker (pronounced Kray-cur) ran a garage known as "White Hart Engineering". . He also had another garage in Roehampton which boasted a telephone number - no such thing was yet available in Chieveley. Another member of the motor trade was Mr. F.Halliday who ran the first bus service between Chieveley Post Office and the Market Place in Newbury, the only means of getting to Newbury other than bicycle or walking or by the Carrier on a Thursday or Saturday..

Mr. Halliday also owned an open topped charabanc with a canvas roof which could be fitted in bad weather and this vehicle carried the villagers to the seaside on the annual outing. There is a picture of one such outing , taken I believe on the seafront at Southsea in 1935 and of which only a few of those pictured survive today. It was not unusual for a person to be born in the village, marry, raise a family and be buried there, without having seen the sea. It was therefore quite an event and a trip to Southsea or some equally far off resort was eagerly looked forward to, everyone struggling to save a few hard earned pennies to be lavished on ice cream (a rare delicacy) and a stroll along the pier. The more daring of the party would put a penny in one of the many "What the butler saw" machines. Quite outrageous in those days and now a much sought after collector's item. The journey home invariably entailed stop at a roadside tavern to spend the remaining few pence, if any, on a drink or two to lubricate the throat. Singing songs of the day was a popular way of passing the time on a journey which was often quite a lengthy, noisy, uncomfortable affair. Eventually many tired but happy folk returned home, full of wonderful memories..

After the services of Mr. Halliday the Newbury & District bus company often referred to as "The Newbury and risk it" ran a daily service in their fleet with its distinctive green and cream livery and in the 1940's the return fare to Newbury was tenpence - four and a half new pence approximately..

CHAPTER NINE

NEXT TO WALNUT Tree cottage and laying back from the road stands a brick built cottage, whose only claim to fame is that it is the birthplace and former home of the writer, and remained so for some twenty five years.

The cottage itself was a very basic affair, boasting two rooms downstairs and two bedrooms above. Cooking was done on a 'Belle' solid fuel kitchen range, which shone brightly due to frequent appliactions of black-lead polish and elbow grease. When it was in a good mood it would produce culinary masterpieces, but with the wind in a north-westerly direction, had the ability to threaten the occupants of the room with suffocation. Other cooking was done on a 'Primus' stove or 'Valor' oil stove. It was not until the 1950's that a second hand electric cooker was purchased, which was a blue and white mottled oven standing on four legs.

. Every drop of water used had to be carried by hand from Coombe House, some 150 yards distance, as and when required, and heated in a copper in a shed opposite the back door. Before the general introduction of a machine, washing day entailed a great deal of hard work for the housewife. Once the water in the copper was heated the clothes would be added, whites washed first to be followed by dark or coloured items. They would be removed from the hot water, using a copper stick. This was a piece of round wood some three feet long and about twice as thick as a broom handle. The washing would then go into a galvanised tub or bath to be rinsed. The next process was to wring out each item by hand to remove excess water, not an easy job with large bed sheets etc. After this, each item would be put through a mangle, two wooden or rubber rollers operated by a handle at one side. This operation removed most of the water after which the week's wash would be pegged out on a line in the garden or draped over a clothes horse in front of the fire during wet weather. The pegs that were used to fix the washing to the line were almost invariably those made by the travelling gypsies, who would offer them for sale to the housewife from a large wicker basket. Also for sale were coloured imitation flowers made from thinly shaved wood together with many other trinkets. The gypsy ladies would call several times a year and would guarantee the buyer good luck if he or she purchased a sprig of "lucky heather". The houswife could have her future predicted by crossing the gypsy's palm with silver, either a little 'joey' (three old pence) or a 'tanner' (six old pence). These gypsies were extremely convincing and often made many accurate predictions.

After drying, ironing would begin, fortunate housewives using an ironing board whilst others made use of the kitchen table. Flat-irons were heated on the fire bars in front of the kitchen range and carefully wiped clean before being applied to the sheets, shirts, table cloths and so on. Very dry clothes would have to be damped with cold water to obtain a smoother result. Semi-stiff collars and shirt fronts were dipped into or sprayed with a solution of starch which gave a crisp finish.

Coppers, as the name suggests were originally constructed of sheet copper but in later years were made of galvanized cast iron, this material being much cheaper. However, it was necessary to have one made of copper when used for the production of home-made wine. I cannot recall the resulting wine ever tasting of the socks or other items of apparel that had been boiling away merrily in the copper the day before

A shed stood opposite the back door in which were a sink and copper, the sink having no water supply. The shed also served as a coal store and bicycle store, whilst the galvanised bath was suspended from a nail driven into the wall. The 'Privy' was part of this shed with a separate outside door, neither place having any form of lighting other than candles or a torch.

The front room of the cottage was not often used except in summer. The open fire in this room was almost as temperamental as the one in the kitchen. In an attempt to get it going, a sheet of newspaper would be held across the opening to increase the draught, which often resulted in the newspaper catching fire. The floor of this room was constructed of very uneven bricks covered in linoleum. The legs of the dining table had to be wedged to get it to stand on an even keel. Because of a lack of damp course the floor was never very dry and it was not unusual for the roots of two poplar trees next to the house to throw up shoots beneath the bookcase which stood in the room. In the kitchen the washing up was done in an enamel bowl on the table, the water being heated by kettle and a handful of washing soda added, this being long before the introduction of washing up liquid and rubber gloves.

Likewise washing and shaving were carried out in a similar manner. In the summer this took place in the shed and in kitchen during the winter. During the 1950's when I started my plumbing business, a second hand sink unit and water heater were fitted and the water supply brought indoors. I can remember my Dad complaining bitterly that I should not have done this, as the property belonged to Mr. Dallin, I also recall, however, that he never again used the sink in the shed for washing and shaving. The bucket type privy was still the only option until the time my mother left the cottage in the 1960's.

The mains water supply was installed in the late 1940's. This work was carried out by Cyril Fry and the service pipe laid from the road to supply a tap in the shed opposite the back door. The trench for this mains supply was dug by hand by my father. At our cottage electricity came in the mid 1930's and consisted of a single light fitting in the centre of the ceiling in each of the four rooms and a single outlet socket in the kitchen. This cottage has been extended and another dwelling erected at the rear on what was originally the kitchen garden.

CHAPTER TEN

Next to the cottage is a field known as the "Coronation Field" which had an area of some 14 acres. This usually held many thoroughbred mares and foals from the adjoining "Middle Farm Stud", owned by Mr. O.W. Rayner of Chieveley Manor.

With the beginning of World War Two, the Stud Farm was closed and the Coronation field let to Weavers. It was still laid down to grass and in 1940 a crop of hay was taken and a rick built in the middle of the field. This was in accordance with a directive from the Ministry of Agriculture that ricks were to be built in the middle of any large flat field, to act as a deterrent should enemy aircraft attempt to land.

The following year the field was ploughed for the first time in living memory and winter oats were sown. In the spring of the following year the crop grew well and reached a height of some five feet or more. Cattle from the adjoining Vicarage Park broke through the hedge and entered the corn field where due to the height of the corn and the large size of the field, they became virtually lost. They did however find the hay rick and due to the somewhat haphazard methods of farming adopted by Weavers, no fence had been placed round the rick. By continually eating around the sides of the rick, it resembled the shape of a mushroom, eventually falling over and suffocating some four of five of the unfortunate beasts. Because of the height of the crop the accident was not discovered for some weeks by which time the stench was unbearable even from a considerable distance. The corn being fit to cut, that left undamaged was then harvested and the remains of the hay rick and the rotting carcases turned into a funeral pyre, much to the dismay of the local dogs who had enjoyed a free supply of meat.

After the war this field became the Recreational Centre with football, cricket and tennis facilities. An ex-Army Nissen hut provided the first pavilion later to be followed by the existing Village Hall. This new hall was erected in 1957 by A.J.Chivers & Son of St. Mary's Hill Newbury, the Architect being John Griffin of Messrs. Sutton, Griffin & Sweetnam, Northbrook Street, Newbury.

The building of this splendid new hall, the envy of many of the local villages was funded partly from local donations, a grant from the "Playing Fields Association" but mainly from a very generous contribution from Mr. Gerald Palmer. The original roof consisted of corrugated asbestos sheeting. Mr. Palmer thought this looked too much like an agricultural building, so it had additional covering of cedar shingles fitted, which greatly improved the visual aspect. Some years later the hall was extended by the addition of changing rooms, toilet facilities, a bar and snooker room. The building has undergone several alterations to the electrical and heating systems and continues to serve the needs of the local community. A badminton club flourished in the 1960's and 70's and now the game of Short Mat bowls is very popular with many people.

At the former Rectory farm a row of houses was erected during the 1970's on the site of the cart horse stables, a large barn, the farmyard and several corrugated grain storage bins. The stables had been accidentally burnt down some years earlier. The site of the last two houses was occupied by a pair of thatched cottages which housed the head carter and his assistant. Part of the original cart shed is still standing and is used as a garden building.

CHAPTER ELEVEN

THE PADDOCK BETWEEN Chieveley Recreational Centre and Middle
Farm was developed as a building site in 2003 and called Middle
Farm Close. The field opposite also now developed and known as
Weavers Place after the former owners of Rectory Farm who used it
as a meadow for their cart horses. All the cart horses used on a farm
had their indiviual names and those at Rectory Farm were' Boxer' a
bay gelding bought from Wyld Court Estates, 'Flower' a grey mare,
'Punch' a grey gelding, son of 'Flower', 'Tinker' a bay gelding who
died in the shafts of a box cart in the Vicarage park, whilst being
driven by myself, and 'Traveller' a liver chestnut gelding almost
uncontrollable, who met his end by lifting the lid of the oat bin in the
stable and gorging himself on the contents. There were other horses
but not so well remembered.

Along the western boundary of the above mentioned horse meadow
adjoining footpath number 10, stood a row of enormous elm trees.
During the early part of the war these were felled by Messrs. Barlows
of Hermitage and the trunks drawn to the saw mill by their team
of six black shire horses. The remaining limbs and branches were
sold to various householders for the sum of ten shillings per tree (50
pence). Each tree top would have yielded several tons of firewood.

This however was long before the days of the chain saw and the wood had to be cut by hand with a bow-saw, the larger pieces being split with metal wedges and finally split to burning-log size with an axe. A daunting task which involved the use of a horse and cart to carry the timber home. I remember my Grandfather having one such treetop and his remarking that he had got heat from it twofold - once when he had to cut and cart it and once when he was sitting by the fire.

Further North on the West side is Pointers Close. The gardens and adjoining land having been developed on what was a chicken farm and known as Freshfields. The owner, Mr. Swepstone was one of the pioneers of the battery system of egg production. Tom Webber from Sunhill made the battery cages from wooden battens and netting wire. They were three cages high and the individual cages measured approximately 18" by 18" by 18", each with its own separate food and water container for the bird. Today's less fortunate birds live in cages only 15" square and share this space with three other birds. Harry Booker ran the chicken farm for Mr. Swepstone and latterly on his own account and lived in the bungalow at the end of Freshfields Lane, the lane and bungalows having previously formed part of the chicken farm. Harry was a great sportsman and played football for Chieveley and was for many years captain of the Cricket Team. His wife Violet was the head cook at Chieveley School.

Opposite Pointer's Close is Middle Farm and its adjoining cottage. This was a stud farm and had an extensive range of loose boxes and exercise paddocks as well as the Coronation field. The stud groom was Frank Bradley. Both he and his wife were avid whist players and attended all the local 'drives'. Their daughter Hilda married Ern Phillips and she played the church organ for many years. The adjoining cottage was home to Harold and Dolly Goodchild, and their sons Sid and Reg.

This site is currently being developed for housing.

Open farm land continued northwards to "Gidley Lane" (BW11) until after the war when a row of bungalows were built and Bardown developed on the remainder of the land. To the south of this site and to the west of Bardown was a very large pit which had been dug many years ago to obtain chalk to be spread on the fields and for other uses. This was one of several in the district, another being in the North Heath road where the sewerage works is situated and another alongside the track from Priors Court road to Curridge (now somewhere in the vicinity of the Main ring on the Showground) and one in the middle of the "Crown Piece". All have been filled in and all trace lost of places which when operational would have involved a massive amount of manual labour.

Adjacent to the footpath to Bardown stands a cottage formerly the home of Mr. Marchant, gardener for Miss Martin-Atkins at Downend House and latterly by his successor Bob Halls. At one time this house was the home of my great grandfather Mr. Barratt who was a boot and shoe maker and plied his trade from these premises.

CHAPTER TWELVE

AT THE JUNCTION with Peasemore road stands the Chestnut tree which at one stage was surrounded by a circular oak seat. This was much used but eventually fell into a state of disrepair and was never replaced.

The Downend council houses, now known as Northfields were completed prior to the Second World War and it was also in the mid 1930's that a mains water supply was installed in the Village, supplied from a borehole and stored in a raised water tank which is now obsolete but is still in position .The village is now supplied from an alternative source.On later ordnance survey maps the Peasemore Road from the chestnut tree has erroneously been shown as Northfields.

Beyond the council houses stands a cottage which was once a very popular shop, owned and run by Miss Rene Bailey. It was a very small shop but carried a vast selection of stock. On her retirement the shop moved across the road, adjoining a new bungalow and continued for many years under the ownership of Mr. John Willoughby and his wife Doris who was Rene Bailey's sister. On their retirement, it became a private house. Bow House, probably so called because of the bay windows on the front elevation, was built by Mr. Box.

He was a relation of Walter Smith and owned and farmed Radnalls Farm. Elm Grove farm and its adjoining cottages stand mid- way between Downend and the junction with what was originally Beedon Common plantation. This farm has been the home of the Smith family for more than fifty years. Walter Smith was a very well respected and knowledgeable man in the equestrian world and annually a British Horse Society stallion would be at stud on the farm, in connection with the hunter improvement scheme which was in force at the time. Walter himself was a very keen huntsman being a member of the Craven Hunt and later with the Vine & Craven after their amalgamation. He was something of a legend in his own time and is reputed to have jumped both the closed gates at Kintbury level crossing in order to keep up with hounds whilst running. The farm has been managed by his two sons Christopher and Peter since his demise. The Vine & Craven Hunt annual point to point races were run at Elm Grove farm for several years. This venue has since moved to Hackwood Park Basingstoke.

The last property on the Peasmore road was known as 'Woods Folly' which has had several owners connected with horses and has recently become home to a racehorse trainer.

CHAPTER THIRTEEN

RETURNING TO THE village and close to the Church is Chieveley Manor, a large house with excellent views of the parkland to the West. This and the adjoining barns and stables were part of the Chieveley Stud owned by Mr. O.W.Rayner, who died in 1929. The Stud continued to function for some years after his death. During his lifetime, Mr.Rayner extended the house by adding the drawing room and extra bedrooms.

The present owners have greatly improved the land and buildings and once again thoroughbred stock is being raised in Chieveley. During the summer months, the annual Chieveley Fete is held in the Manor gardens, and the gardens are open to the public on certain days in conjunction with the National Gardens Scheme.

Braziers Farm house which stands opposite Church Lane, and the properties in the opposite corner were built at the same time and the design and use of materials is very similar. "Homelea" now "The Chase" which is situated near the entrance to Church Lane was for many years the home of Mr. W. Pocock who was a Prudential Assurance agent. After that Cyril Fry, son the local blacksmith married Lily daughter of Mr. Pocock and moved in, where he started a plumbing business. At that time the mains supply had become available and a lot of work was generated. He employed Reg Crook from Yattendon who was a keen church bellringer and Reg took over the business on Cyril's retirement and he continued until the mid 1950's, when I started a plumbing and heating business known as Martin of Chieveley, operating from a workshop and store in Manor Lane (Pig Lane). This business flourished and employed several local men until my retirement in 1995.

Over this period vast changes took place in the plumbing trade. Government grants became available for home improvement schemes and most houses were fitted with bathrooms and hot water systems. Traditional lead and iron pipes disappeared to be replaced with copper, asbestos and plastic, these materials being much easier and quicker to install. Also, pumped small bore heating systems were developed together with oil fired boilers which increased the work load but certainly helped to reduce the usual spate of bursts due to frost. When starting work in January 1944 I was paid the grand sum of fifteen shillings (75p) for a week of forty seven and a half hours, cycling to and from Newbury and then often cycling on to places as far afield as Kintbury, Thatcham, Kingsclere and Stockcross to the current place of work. Today, one hears of charges of £70 an hour and more often than not a "call out" fee, which was unheard of in my days..

In the High Street, stands the Village Shop and Bakery started at the beginning of the century by the Shepherd family, Mr. W.H.Shepherd followed by his sons Wally and Stan and Bill (not in the business) and then in later years, Wally's son Andrew and his sisters, Judith and Gillian. This shop was a very thriving enteprise in the 40's and 50's, delivering groceries and bread over a wide area to the neighbouring villages. The Post Office was incorporated into the Shop in later years.

On leaving school in August 1944, in common with a goodly number of other fourteen year olds, I had no idea what I wanted to do as a job of work. Before I knew it, I had acquired two jobs, in the mornings I went "into service" at Coombe House where my duties were general household work, bed-making, polishing, dusting and my most hated of all jobs, that of scrubbing the back stairs. These were of plain wood and were scrubbed with a stiff brush, using a bucket of water and a bar of carbolic soap. I still hate every one of those fifteen stairs.

My afternoons were taken up working for Shepherd's as a delivery boy, taking bread and groceries to customers in the village. For this purpose I used a trade bicycle complete with a large basket mounted at the front. This was fine during good weather but on several occasions I well recall using a home made sledge to transport the deliveries when deep snow made cycling impossible. Another task was in the dry goods store, weighing up various items such as rice, lentils, peas, beans and chicken feed of several sorts. All these commodities were delivered in bulk sacks and had to be packaged into brown paper bags of various weights for sale in the shop. Having realised that both these jobs were something of a dead end I left them both at the end of the year. It was about this time that I made the decision to change my name. Having always been called Willie, I decided that Bill would sound a bit more grown up, so the change was made but took a considerable time to achieve in some quarters. Since then of course I have been known by various names, some not altogether polite. After a none too ambitious start to my working life, my first proper employer was E. Lipscombe & Sons, Plumbers of Oxford Street, Newbury. I obtained this job in response to an advertisement in the Newbury Weekly News. The cost of the insertion would have been priced per word and merely stated "Strong lad wanted for building trade". Little did I realise that this would lead to my continuing in the plumbing trade for the next fifty one years.

CHAPTER FOURTEEN

ONE OF SHEPHERD'S roundsmen, van driver Ted Cox was a real character, whose hobby was testing home made wine. At the end of some delivery rounds it was fortunate that the roads were not as busy as they are today although one van at least was written off. Another attribute of Ted's was that of a butcher and during the war years most Saturday afternoons in the winter, I would accompany him, killing pigs for people as in those days many pigs were kept in sties at the bottom of the garden, where they would be fed on kitchen scraps, potatoes etc. In some cases an allocation of pig food could be applied for and was obtained with a licence from the Government, with the proviso that half the carcase would be claimed by them when the animal was slaughtered. In a good many cases however, the pig owners were employed by the local farmer and often 'perks' obtained in the form of turnips, mangels etc were used to help feed their pigs.

One particular day we were due to kill a couple of pigs for a man who lived in one of a row of cottages on the Bothampstead Road at Worlds End. This road became a dead-end when the A34 was re-routed. The usual method of holding a pig was by a cord some three feet in length with a loop at one end. This noose was placed over the upper jaw and the cord wound round the lower jaw and snout. On this day, our intended victim managed to struggle free and forced a way through the garden hedge, crossed the road and negotiated another hedge into the field beyond. It ran across two further fields before being recaptured near Langley Wood, some half a mile from the start. It took the combined efforts of three men and a boy (me) to return the poor creature to its point of execution.

This was carried out in a very humane manner. The animal would first be stunned with a captive bolt pistol which fired a steel pin approximately the size of a pencil directly into the animal's brain. Its' throat would then be laid open and the jugular vein severed. Occasionally a housewife who specialised in making black pudding would ask for the blood to be saved for this purpose. Next came the removal of the bristle which covered the pig. The carcase would be covered with dry straw which was then ignited. Too little straw would not burn the bristle and too much would damage the skin of the pig. When one side was done the carcase was turned over and the operation repeated. A sharp knife was then used much in the style of a cut-throat razor to remove any remaining bristle. This process was used on any carcase to be cured for bacon. If the animal was to be used as pork, the bristles were removed with very hot water, usually carried from the copper in the wash house and poured over the pig with a wooden handled galvanised dipper. The bristle would then be scraped off, leaving a clean almost white skin.

A 'W' shaped hook would be inserted into the tendons of the hind legs just above the hock and then with a rope attached to this hook, the carcase was hoisted up over the branch of a suitable tree or beam in the roof of a shed. The entrails and offal were removed and carefully set aside to be processed for eating.

Ted Cox would then go back the next day to joint the carcase, either for curing as bacon, or to be eaten as fresh pork, there being no deep freezers at that time. Nothing was ever wasted and bears out the old saying that 'the only part of the pig which can't be eaten is the grunt'. Seldom seen today, many pig keepers had a heavy stool or table on which the carcase was placed for butchering. These stools were usually a heavy plank of wood some four to five feet in length and about one foot six inches in width. It would be supported by four stout legs and stood about two feet from the ground. Many such stools were used as garden seats in the summer time, as pig killing generally took place during the winter months.

CHAPTER FIFTEEN

MY GRANDFATHER, FRED Leach, was baker at Shepherds and his day started at 6 am but on Saturdays this was brought forward to 3 am so that the bread could be produced and delivered to allow the delivery van to be available to transport the local football team to their away fixtures.

In those days Chieveley had a very strong team, one year winning the Reading Town Senior.Cup, played on Elm Park then the home of Reading F.C.

The original bakehouse was built in white glazed bricks with a tiled floor and the ovens were fired by coke from a stoke hole at the rear. This form of heating was changed to oil in the 1960's. Another bakehouse was added during the early part of the war, enabling the output to be doubled. At the rear of this bakehouse stood a row of sheds and pig sties, the pigs living mainly on stale bread, also an outside privy that boasted a three hole seat, two large and one small, all these amenities being next to the bakehouse. Beyond the building and the churchyard hedge was an orchard, later built on to provide a house for Andrew Shepherd and his family. The family grocery shop of Shepherds was sold on to new owners and has changed hands several times since. At the time of the original sale the petrol pumps that stood at the front of the shop on the North corner were removed thus relieving the High Street of a certain amount of congestion. The Shepherd family retained the bakehouse and ran it as a wholesale bakery, supplying many outlets in the retail and catering trade over a large area.

Wally Shepherd was a real village character and would spend much of his time seated in his office on the telephone, taking grocery orders for delivery by the roundsman. He would ring many of his customers with enticing offers and inform them which items were particularly good that week. What I wonder would be his reaction to today's technology with customers shopping 'on line' and having their goods delivered to the door at the click of a mouse. Another fond memory I have of Wally was during our days together singing in the Church Choir in the 1950's when often after having processed up the aisle to our seats in the Choir, Wally would realise that he had left his glasses at home. I would then have to leave the Church by way of the Vicar's vestry and rush to the shop, hunt for the missing spectacles and hope to back in Church in time for the second hymn. He was also somewhat inquisitive in Church and would often ask in a very loud voice 'Who is that?' should a strange face be in the congregation.

The next house to the Shop is Sowbury House, for many years the home of Mrs Wintour and her companion Miss Hopson. On the wall of the building on the right of the entrance gateway, stood a peach tree, which was Mrs Wintour's pride and joy. A glass roof on cantilver brackets was fixed above it and the fruit netted in the summer. Each fruit would be suspended in a muslin bag until ripe. All and sundry passing by were invited in to admire the crop but I cannot recall ever having an invitation to taste it. Strangely it always survived the longing looks of passing schoolboys, none of whom would think twice about scrumping apples, plums or nuts. Also fixed to the same wall as the peach tree was a water clock. This was made of lead and highly decorated. A reservoir at the top was filled with water to allow the clock to operate although I don't remember how we told the time from it.

The garden of Sowbury House was large affair, again forming a boundary with the Church yard and Sowbury path (footpath no.1

from the Churchyard to School Road). This was planted with fruit trees at the beginning of the war, but the house having changed hands several times the garden was sold off for building with access from Sowbury Park,. Likewise the garden between the house and the old Post Office was used for a similar purpose.

CHAPTER SIXTEEN

Opposite, on the East side of the High Street stands Chieveley House. This house was used as a Land Army hostel during the war years and housed a large number of Land Girls. This fact, combined with American Servicemen at Hermitage Camp and Welford made Chieveley a very popular place and ensured that all the public houses and local dances were well supported. The house has undergone many changes under the ownership of several distinguished persons. The garden has been enlarged and enclosed and admired by all, especially in late May of each year when the Church annual Plant Sale is held in the grounds. The extension to the garden entailed the re-alignment of the Back Alley, path number 2, and the extra ground was enclosed by a concrete block wall erected by Tommy Hall and Reg Williams. A plaque bearing their names and the time of construction is placed in the wall. At the time it was known as Chieveley's answer to the Berlin Wall or the Great Wall of Chieveley. Over the years it has mellowed and with judicious tree planting now blends in remarkably well with the surroundings.

On the West side of the High Street is the Old Post Office,which served the village for many years before transferring to the village shop. The Old Post Office also housed a manually operated telephone exchange, run by Dick Cann's mother and his sister Joan. A few early numbers that I remember were of the single figure variety the Manor - 8, New Farm 6, Prismall's 7, Coombe House 5, Shepherd's shop 14 all of these now being preceded by five digits plus another five digits for the area code.

Postal deliveries were made by a Postman, resplendent in his blue uniform and peaked cap and riding a red bicycle with a carrier on the front. Chieveley had two full time postmen, the earliest I can rember was Mr. Jimmy Holmes. He lived at The Firs, now demolished, by the Chestnut Tree and his wife taught at the school. Also living in Down End was a Mr. Holliday. Later the job was taken on by Tom Winter who lived at Rectory Farm Cottages, also now demolished, and latterly in Horsemoor. He shared the job with Harold Goodchild, Reg's father, who lived at Middle Farm. Then came Wesley Leach, Derek's father, who lived in Down End and Jack Winter who lived in Pointers Bungalow before moving to Manor Lodge and becoming gardener at the Manor. He now lives in Kintbury.

These stalwarts did a tremendous job, for although cycling on their rounds in the summer may have been a pleasant occupation, trudging round on foot with a heavy mail bag in deep snow was an entirely different matter. Also in those days I cannot recall a winter without snow. In the late 1970's it snowed on Boxing Day and had not gone until almost April. Mail was generally delivered on time and was certainly good value at 2d a letter and 1d for postcards.

CHAPTER SEVENTEEN

Next to the Old Post Office is The Forge where Ted Fry operated as a blacksmith and farrier, travelling round the local farms shoeing horses. Rumour has it that his wife had to untie the old white pony and trap from the railings in front of the Wheatsheaf Pub often late at night and take him home. It is said that after working at an outlying farm, he was often lifted into the trap and the pony found its own way home. As schoolboys we spent many hours watching Ted at work in the Smithy with the clang of hammer on red hot iron and sparks flying in all directions. A particularly fascinating sight was to watch red hot metal rims being shrunk on to wagon and carriage wheels.

Ted Fry or Teddy as he was always known, was not a large brawny man, the type often associated with blacksmithing. In fact he was quite small and wiry with a drooping walrus type moustache and seldom seen without his flat cap and leather apron.

The Smithy was a very dark and gloomy building, with the roof timbers blackened with the soot from the forge, whilst the walls were hung with hundreds of horse shoes of many shapes and sizes, ranging from the very smallest for donkeys or Shetland ponies to the very largest for the mighty Shires, these being almost as large in diameter as a dinner plate. Long lengths of iron bar and rod of all sizes cluttered the floor, scarcely leaving room for his faithfull old dog to find room to rest. In spite of the general mayhem and the fact that even in bad weather, horses brought to the forge for shoeing were shod in the open, Ted never seemed to mind us boys hanging around even if we did happen to get in his way. As school boys an unforgettable sight for us was Ted crouched beneath a massive Shire horse, fitting a horse-shoe with the resultant clouds of steam and smoke issuing from the burning hoof horn, and what to us was a frequent event can now been seen by today's young generation possibly at annual agricultural shows or country fairs.

When Teddy Fry retired the business closed, his son Cyril having set up as a plumber. Dick Cann used the site as a builder's yard, eventually moving into the house and he is responsible for building many of the houses that form Chieveley today, especially Heathfields in School Road. This building business employed a large number of local men and in addition to building houses, carried out contract joinery work. Unlike some village builders their services did not include undertaking. This work was done in the adjoining villages of Brightwalton by H & G Wells & Sons and in Hermitage by R. Burgess & Son. These firms made their own coffins from "coffin boards" cut from the trunk of a large elm tree and stocked by Messrs. Barlows, Timber Merchants of Long Lane. A few 'boxes' of standard size would be kept in stock by the Undertakers. Should, however the deceased be too large or too small, a suitably sized coffin would be made in the workshop to be completed at very short notice. The elm boards were approximately one inch thick, twenty four inches wide and six feet six inches long. To form the taper at either end, the inner part of the wallboard was partially sawn through at intervals of approximately one inch, to allow the wood to be bent to fit the shape of the base. The whole thing was then nailed together and a pre-formed moulding fitted to cover the nail heads. Next, liquid pitch would be used to coat the inside and a fabric lining fitted, with folds to cover the body. A small white pillow stuffed with sawdust was also placed under the head. The lid was screwed on and polished handles, usually brass, fitted to each side. The name plate would often be handwritten and affixed to the lid. As well as making the coffin, the builders' employees would also dig the grave, act as bearers, fill in the grave after the ceremony, return to the yard, change into their working clothes and get on with the job in hand.

As cremations became more popular, the coffins were mass produced in a factory from veneered chipboard and the fittings made of plastic. All this to make them totally combustible. Not like the old style 'boxes' which were made to last.

CHAPTER EIGHTEEN

NEXT TO THE Forge are two cottages and then the Methodist Chapel, erected in 1914 on land given by Mr. Rayner. This is now a dwelling house but apart from normal Chapel services, was home at one time to the "Band of Hope and the "Chieveley Harmonica Band"

The "Band of Hope" Chieveley branch was formed in the early years of the war. Hammonds sweet shop was taken over by Miss Agent who together with her friend Miss Nance Allen and Mr. and Mrs. Davis started this venture and most of the youngsters of the village were encouraged to sign the pledge, to refrain from the temptations and evils of strong drink. Many tales were told and sketches performed to impress upon the young the dangers of alcohol. I have often wondered how many remained loyal to their Pledge. As a backslider, I regret that my promises in that regard came to nought. During the summer this same team from the Chapel also arranged evening picnics. This was a mixed affair for boys and girls and a party would set off to a given spot within walking distance, for example Bussock or Bradley Wood, build a fire and cook sausages to be eaten with chunks of Shepherd's bread. No thought seemed to be given to the moral risks of such gatherings but in those days teenagers developed much later than their counterparts of today. One particular instance which comes to mind involved a picnic in Bradley Wood. A small fire had been lighted to cook the food but due to the abundance of fallen dead branches, the blaze reached such proportions that it became dangerous and it was decided that the best way to put it out would be for the young men in the party to use natural methods to douse the flames, the young ladies being asked meanwhile to retire to a suitable distance. This proved to be a successful operation, but the panic caused amongst the organisers made this the last venture of its kind.

The "Chieveley Harmonica Band" was the brainchild of the Misses Elsie and Eva Sadler who lived at The Mount, both devout Methodists. This being the case the schoolroom at the rear of the Chapel, became the venue for the Band's rehearsals. There must have been a dozen or so members, all equipped with various sizes and types of mouth-organ, all of which had numbers on the mouthpiece. The tune being played was by numbers rather than by notes on a musical stave. The standard of performance never reached a particular high and I cannot recall any public outing. Alas the group disbanded probably with the coming of the light summer evenings, and the need for its members to indulge in the age old pursuits of birds nesting, tree climbing and so forth. Some of the lads of my age were at that time members of the Church Choir and none to my knowledge ever attended the regular services at the Chapel.However, we always seemed to go carol singing round the village with the Chapel and Miss Sadler played a small portable organ, which the boys carried. On one particular night, after trudging round the village and Downend, she decided to go to Bow House, some half a mile towards Peasemore. Those of us carrying the organ felt that this would be too far, so the organ was left under the Chestnut tree and we, the carriers, went home. (Perhaps it's still there). Sadly with the decline in numbers of congregation at the Chapel and the increasing age of those able to attend, the Chapel closed in the 1960's. It stood empty for some years and was eventually purchased by Mr. Bill Pearce the builder who used it as a store. It has now been transformed into a dwelling house.

Opposite the Chapel in the house called Woodlands, lived Mr. Inman Taylor who ran a wholesale egg business which was a forerunner of a firm called Thames Valley Poultry Producers. In a building adjoining the house, the eggs were in large wooden crates which were piled from floor to ceiling, and as children we wondered where so many eggs came from as most people kept a few hens of their own which provided the eggs for their needs or purchased them from one of the many smallholdings in the village..

CHAPTER NINETEEN

AGAIN ALMOST OPPOSITE the Chapel is the "Old Infant School" now called 'The Old Schoolhouse'. This school was built in 1865 together with its adjoining cottage. This was where the village children had their lessons, following the closure of the schoolroom at North Heath and until the opening of the new School in School road, built in 1897. The old school and adjoining cottage is now one dwelling but during the war was the headquarters of the local "Home Guard". Tom Phillips, Landlord of the Hare & Hounds was, together with the rest of the troop, some twenty men, cleaning rifles. Tom's rifle had one "up the spout" and the bullet from the discharge made a dent in the brickwork above the fireplace, hit the ceiling and then buried itself in the floor. There were no casualties, nor were there any more accidents.

On another occasion, several members of the Home Guard were practising throwing 'Mills' hand grenades from a specially built trench at Hazelhanger on the site of a former gravel works. The thrower pulled the pin and in attempting to throw the grenade, caught his hand on a sandbag and dropped the grenade. With only a six second delay it could have proved disastrous for the rest of the men in the trench.. Thanks to quick thinking and the prompt action of one

Sargeant Lambert (cow-man at Priors Court Farm) he grabbed the grenade and tossed it out of the trench where it exploded harmlessly ,thus avoiding a tragedy.

The Old Infant School room was for a time during the latter part of the war ,the headquarters of Chieveley Army Cadets. They numbered some ten to twelve members and were trained by a serving soldier, a Sergeant who arrived each week in a Hillman pick-up truck. This vehicle was also used to transport the unit to Shefford where we held joint exercises with their troop We became very proficient at arms drill, with rifles that were not operable and also learned map reading. One or two joint parades took place in Newbury with this Troop and members of the Sea Cadets and the Air Training Corps. All this training prepared us for National Service, which was to follow on reaching the age of eighteen. Most of the group were called up and served in many parts of the world in one or other of the three armed services.

Another memory of my Army Cadet days was the annual camp which consisted of a week spent under canvas - one year at Tweasledown Racecourse and another at Mychett, both near Aldershot. The highlights of the week being a visit to the ranges where we were allowed to fire live ammunition. On arrival at the camp each individual was provided with a palliasse which had to be filled with straw (this having been used for the same purpose on many previous occasions by other units). Another task was to dig a slit trench into which the cadet jumped on hearing the air-raid warning,this being the time when the German V-one bombers were making regular sorties against Britain. They could be heard passing over head followed by an ominous silence when they ran out of fuel, this being followed by an almighty explosion on impact. Although these raids were quite frequent we were never very near to their point of landing. It is nevertheless quite a memorable experience to be one of ten lads sleeping in a bell tent all desperately trying to find the exit flap in the middle of the night and in pitch darkness. Also having found one's slit trench to discover it already occupied.

Another vivid recollection of my career in the Army Cadets was an occurrence during the months of April and May in 1944. During the build up to the D-Day Airborne Invasion of Normandy, Welford

Camp was the base for many B-47 Dakotas and several hundred troop-carrying gliders. Dressed in our Army Cadet uniform and armed with a note giving parental permission, Eric Napper, myself and several other young teenagers would cycle to Welford on a Sunday (after Church) and then have flights in the Dakotas as they towed their gliders into the sky for release on training flights. Most days we would have four or five such flights each lasting some thirty to forty minutes, usually followed by tea in the US Army mess.

There were two main types of glider at Welford, first the large Horsa of which many were made in Newbury by Elliots the furniture manufacturers at their Albert Road factory, now the site of the Bayer Company. Elliots was owned by the Buckingham brothers and prior to the war in addition to manufacturing furniture, they also produced a small private glider called the "Eon" this name being derived from the firm's title "Elliots of Newbury". The military gliders were built there and transported to the various airfields for assembly. The second type of glider based at Welford was the "Waco" another rather ugly blunt nosed machine produced in America by the Ford Motor Company and the components shipped over here and assembled on site. This glider was somewhat smaller than the Horsa and the Dakota B-47 would often tow two of them at the same time. The large wooden crates in which the glider components had made their transatlantic crossing seemed to appear in all sorts of places, especially on farms and in gardens as they made ideal garages or housing for livestock. There was of course in those days no permission required for such an erection. There was another American glider called the "Hadrian" but I do not recall seeing any of these at Welford. During their training period the US forces would often land by glider in the fields around Chieveley, North Heath and Winterbourne, the gliders wings were then dismantled and the whole machine returned to base on low-loading trailers, similar to those used by the RAF and often referred to as "Queen Marys" (after the Liner) due to their width and their length of some sixty feet,which could take up most of the width of our narrow country roads.

These glider landings and the many thousands of paratroopers taking part in exercises left a vast amount of 'souvenirs' for the local lads to find - American service torches, unopened 'K' rations, often live ammunition and various items of kit were much sought after by the youth of the villages. The female sex were often seen sporting white nylon scarves made from parachute material. I know not whether any items of clothing were made from the same material but from the construction of the parachute it was not possible to obtain remnants of any great size.

It was an amazing sight to watch the paratroops training for active service. Often as many as thirty or so Dakotas would fly over the dropping zone in the Chieveley area, each discharging some twenty five to thirty paratroops at almost the same time. The sky would be filled with hundreds of camoflaged parachutes, each with its human cargo or container of equipment. One sees from war-time films that many of these gliders made horrendous landings in Europe but although they may have ploughed through hedges or lost wings in collision with trees, I do not recall hearing of any fatal crashes occuring during the training period that took place locally. A tense atmosphere among the Americans was building up prior to the invasion and the whole of our area as indeed most of the South of England took on the proportions of one huge military encampment. Just before the invasion all the planes and gliders taking part had large white identification stripes painted on their wings and bodies. Seemingly overnight everything became very quiet. This however proved to be very brief interlude, as within a few days the local roads were very busy with ambulances ferrying the wounded who had been brought back from France, to Welford and Greenham, for treatment at the US Military Hospital at Hermitage. Little did any of the personnel know at that time, that during the Cold War in later years Welford Base and Greenham Common would become the home of nuclear missiles and a large force of US Military personnel, or that Greenham would become well known world wide because of the actions of the Peace Campaigners..

CHAPTER TWENTY NINE

Continuing our journey through Chieveley village, the property next to the Old Infant School was home for many years to Leon and Violet Webber, long serving Organists at the Church. Prior to their being in this property it was a tobacconists and newsagents run by Mr. and Mrs. Hammond. Mr. Hammond also owned and ran a smallholding on the site now occupied by the Newbury Agricultural Society office.

Freddy 'Major' Hammond always rode a bicycle with a carrier on the front, between his home at the shop and his smallholding. He also had a car available for hire but I cannot recall ever seeing him driving this vehicle.

This shop was mainly responsible for giving the class of 1935 at Chieveley School the opportunity to purchase 5 Woodbine cigarettes, a box of matches and a two ounce paper bag of aniseed balls (to disguise the tobacco smell) all for the sum of five pennies.

Next we come to "The Square" which of course is not a square but a triangle. This I suppose must be considered the centre of the Village. At one time a pond was situated on the South side, but was filled in some time in the late 1920's. On the East side stood "The Wheatsheaf" recently turned into a house, and at the rear of the pub off the footpath No. 2 , known as the Back Alley, to East Lane, is a field which for many years was the home of Chieveley Football Club. The teams changed in a shed at the back of the pub and occasionally a bucket of tepid water was made available to the visiting team after the match to allow them to leave the Chieveley soil behind. The home team had to be content to take it home with them. Quite often the cattle had to be driven off to another field to allow the game to start and so it was often not only mud that was collected by the participants. After the move to the Chieveley Recreation Ground, hot showers became available, a licensed bar and other home comforts. This however did nothing to improve the standard of play and a gradual decline of the Club set in.

The Wheatsheaf has seen many changes of Landlord over the years. The earliest I recollect being Dolly Shefford and then Bill and Mrs. Crawford who ran it for many years both during and after the war. It has now become a private house but it is nice to note that the Morlands Brewery emblem of an artist has been retained at the side of the main entrance.

The Square has seen many festive occasions especially VE and VJ night celebrations. I remember a visit and performance by the Vancouver Boys Band, although I think they may have played at a few other venues besides Chieveley.

Another sight was four fully loaded double decker buses to transport Chieveley Football Club supporters to Newbury for the final of the Greystone Cup on the Newbury ground. There were not too many people left in Chieveley that afternoon. Although I recall this sight I do not remember who our opponents were or the outcome of the game.

On the South side of the Square stands the "The Limes" with an adjoining cottage, stable and other buildings. This was owned Mr. D. West, who ran a coal and coke business together with a depot at Hermitage Station. He also owned a meadow and orchard near Church Farm. An outstanding feature at The Limes was an enormous Aucuparia or monkey puzzle tree which stood in the garden at the front of the house alongside a path which ran from the front door to a gate opening into School Road. This impressive tree must have been some forty to fifty feet in height.

After the Wests came Herbert Prismall who owned and ran the grocers and bakers business in High Street, almost opposite Coombe House. In the late 1930's Trotmans the butchers opened a shop in that part of The Limes facing the Square, and this in turn was taken over after the war by Mr. Willner who continued to run it as such, until his retirement in the 1990's and until the coming of the supermarket sounded the death knell for most village butchers. Gerhardt Frederich Willner had been a German seaman and served in U-boats at the beginning of World War 2. After his capture he remained in this country and at the end of the war, took over the village butchers, he soon built up a good trade with his home cooked fare, much of which had a distinctly continental flavour. Since beginning these memoirs the stable and loft building of the butchers have been partially demolished following an accident involving a motor vehicle. It is noted that at the time of the occurrence, the building was stationary. Traffic is currently being controlled by traffic lights and causes great frustration to the local road users. The loft above the stable (also damaged) used to be the site of a game played by Eric Napper, who lived in the adjoining cottage, Geoffrey Howe, myself and others who gathered in the loft in semi-darkness, as it had no windows, and then take turns in attempting to extinguish the flame of a candle by firing at it with an air-gun.

CHAPTER THIRTY

ON THE HIGHER ground next to "The Wheatsheaf" is "The Mount" at one time home to the two Misses Sadler, who were the leading lights at the Methodist Chapel. At this Chapel my Grandmother was in the congregation when the usual organist failed to appear and she was asked to play. She made a mistake, turned round to apologize to the assembled company, saying that she was a bit out of practice. This was some weeks after her ninety second birthday. She had not played the organ for at least the past ten years and the Methodist Chapel instrument was an harmonium which had to be operated by foot pedals not an easy task for a lady of her age coupled with the fact that she was no more than five feet tall. Before this and until she was in her mid-seventies, she regularly played the organ each Sunday at World's End Chapel. During the winter months she was usually offered transport but in the summer always made the journey on foot from Horsemoor to World's End, by way of Morphett's Lane and footpaths across the fields.

Following the Miss Sadlers, Miss Cranfield lived at the Mount. She was a retired headmistress and an extremely charming lady who took a leading role in many of the village's social activities. Regrettably, due to a typographical error, her obituary in the Parish

Magazine in the late 1950's referred to her as being 'a very pubic spirited person'.

Next is a row of three cottages backing onto the road.. On the North end of the row is another Back Alley (FP no.3) which emerges at the rear of the Red Lion Public House. On the opposite side of the road stood a row of three cottages called Folly Cottages, now demolished and a house built called.Rothbury House..

Next to this house is a former shop known as The Folly Stores which was run by Miss Rose Robinson. This business operated until the 1950's when, on her retirement, it became a private house, now known as The Folly. Next door at number 1 Makina Villas lived Dougie and Grace Warmingham who ran the local Newsagents after the closure of Hammonds shop. At number 2 Makina Villas lived the Pearce family, another well known local family. Son Frank also ran a newspaper delivery service in the village, before the Warminghams took over .Frank and his wife then later had the Sunway Transport Cafe which was sited just past the Langley Hall pub at Worlds End where the trading estate now stands.

CHAPTER THIRTY ONE

ON THE OTHER side of Graces Lane, named after a former Chieveley resident Mr. John Grace,who died in 1816, stands Chapel Cottage. This former Wesleyan Chapel was converted to a house immediately after the war by Dick Cann for Mr. and Mrs. D.Saint. 'Dougie' Saint taught history and woodwork at St. Bartholomew's Boys' Grammar School, leaving at the commencement of the war to join the Royal Air Force, becoming Squadron Leader. He returned to the school and eventually was deputy headmaster. Mrs. Dora Saint taught for a good number of years at Chieveley School, later becoming a celebrity as author of the "Miss Read" series of books. Perhaps the source of some of these stories may have been based on her experiences whilst teaching at Chieveley. Mr. and Mrs. Saint subsequently moved to Wickham.

Next a pair of thatched cottages, now known as Well Cottage. Next is Lilac Cottage which was built as a School in the late 1700's and called a Dame School and taught between ten and twenty pupils. It is fair to assume that it ceased as a school when the new infant school opened in the High Street in 1865, that having some seventy pupils.

In the early 1930's numbers 1 - 6 Council Houses were built, later known as Southfields . Over the years these have housed well known village families, the Belchers, the Lawrences, the Bosleys and Knights. The land opposite these houses was developed during the 1960's - one house being constructed for the local Nurse.The last house but one on the South side of Graces Lane, now called Blackthorn Cottage, was built and lived in by Ern Taylor and his wife who had been the District Nurse for many years. Ern had been a part time builder. When well into his seventies and many years before pre-mixed concrete had been invented, Ern was invited by farmer John Weaver to let him have a price to lay a concrete road from Church Farm to New Sheds (approximately 300 yards),. a major undertaking for a single handed builder, particularly of his age. Expecting a written estimate, Farmer Weaver was surprised to be told "I'll let you have it now -£20 more than Dick Cann's price".

Beyond these houses and somewhere in the position of the bridge over the A34 on the Priors Court Road was the original "crossroads" and even as far back as the 1950's it often took some time to cross the A34 to get to Hermitage due to the volume of traffic, particularly during the main holiday weeks during the summer when the majority of the factories in the Midlands closed for their annual holiday, and many made their way to the resorts on the South Coast for sun, sea and sand,. the A34 being the main trunk road from North to South before the advent of motorways.

During the war the slightly higher ground in the North west corner was fortified by the Home Guard with several trenches and gun positions as this site gave remarkable views of the surrounding roads in all directions. The main Oxford road (A34) was years ago referred to as "The Turnpike". As tolls were levied on the large flocks of sheep travelling to and from East Ilsley Sheep Fair, to avoid paying these tolls many flocks were driven by way of North Heath and Old Street as a form of by-pass.

CHAPTER THIRTY TWO

PRIORS COURT HOUSE has had a long and varied history and belonged in the writer's time, early 1930's, to Mr. Eustace Exall Palmer of the Huntley & Palmer Biscuit manufacturing company. During the the early part of the war the Chieveley Womens' Institute met in the Drawing Room where sewing and knitting were carried out to provide "comforts" for the troops. Chieveley Cricket Club played their home matches at Priors Court and were the envy of most of their opposing teams for this was one of the very few pitches in those days that could boast a mown outfield. Most other villages had a narrow strip of prepared wicket, the rest of the outfield being ordinary pasture. Many a six was run with the ball lying only a few yards from the stumps and until one of the fielding side called "Lost ball!" The Chieveley Cricket Club was largely comprised of Priors Court Staff who all lived in the row of staff cottages. They were Billy Jones-Chauffeur, Walter Hadlow - Butler, Bill Rout - Gardener, Arthur Harkness - Footman, together with Bill Aubury and Bill Roberts.

A tale often told by Ed "Slip" Leach, another cricketer, concerns the day that he hit a ball so high that it looked like a "Beechams Pill" and that six runs were completed before it came down to earth where it buried itself so deep in the outfield that a spade had to be called for in order to retrieve it.

When Kingswood School took over the Court as a junior school at the beginning of the war, the Cricket Club lost the use of the ground and next moved to a field at New Farm Chieveley, which is now Sowbury Park. After several years there, they played on the "Rec" opposite the School, a ground which proved to be rather small. Their final move to the Recreation Centre took place in the late 1950's.

Kingswood Junior School moved to the Main school in Bath in the late 1990's and Priors Court is now the home, after much improvement, for children with special needs.

Beyond Priors Court cottages, towards Hermitage village, stood Priors Court Farm which was a dairy and arable farm and this included the land now occupied by the Agricultural Society and land towards Bradley Court. This farm was run by Mr. Carter. The farm was demolished at the time the M4 was constructed and the site of the farm buildings are now occupied by a pallet company.

The two farm bungalows still remain, one being occupied by Len Povey whose family originally lived in the council houses at Downend. With the coming of the M4 motorway, the Hermitage road was diverted over what is now the new bridge. The old road still serves another pair of cottages to the East of the motorway. Adjoining these is a Horticltural business . Next we have a house formerly known as The Crundel which is now a Childrens' Nursery "Acres of Fun". Beyond the turning to Oare is Hilliers's Garden Centre. This was originally started by Mr. Tuersley in the 1970's.

Still in Chieveley Parish is Hermitage Camp built hurriedly during the second world war as a hospital for wounded American personnel. It consisted of a large number of wards, together with operating theatres and accommodation units, all connected by external covered walkways and with its own water supply system fed from a large storage tank about twenty metres high, sited adjacent to Priors Court road. . This hospital worked in conjunction with other local American bases, which were situated at Greenham Common (Aircraft) Welford (Aircraft and Gliders), Newbury Racecourse (Stores) Snelsmore Common (Fuel Dump). Chieveley being situated in the centre of this triangle, together with the attraction of a Land Army hostel at Chieveley House, three public houses and numerous dances in the village hall, Chieveley is possibly a name very well known in many parts of the USA.

Hermitage Camp became a resettlement unit for members of the Polish Armed Forces after the end of the war. The British Army (Royal Engineers) then extended the Camp adding many new buildings including married quarters. This unit became known as the School of Military Survey.

CHAPTER THIRTY THREE

FROM THE RED Lion public house in the village, Green Lane runs in a Southerly direction and is reputed to have once been the main road to Newbury. Before the building of the M4 motorway this Lane ran towards Bussock Wood, (BW 7) and then crossed the A34 just South of Sevenacres and continued on to Curridge as Chalky Lane (BW no.36) . Another branch ran through Bussock Wood (FP no.9) past part of the corner of the Wood known as the Parsons's Acre to Snelsmore Farm, whilst skirting the wood on the North side another footpath ran along the Northern edge of the wood to cross the Wantage road at Bussock Mayne and continued on to Winterbourne as BW's 5 and 5a.

A corner of Bussock Wood has always been known as The Parsons's Acre. This was formed by the footpaths at the East and Northern sides and the Southwest corner marked by a large sarsen stone. It was always believed that this acre of land belonged to the Church but latterly I understand it was so called because the Vicar of the time had coppicing rights to it. However with the coming of the M4 motorway, Bussock Wood is completely isolated from Chieveley, except for the footbridge which is approached from Chieveley fields. This bridge has been upgraded to a bridle way in connection with the major improvements and underpass scheme at Junction 13 of the M4. A magnificent structure has now replaced the old footbridge and should prove an asset to local horse riders.

The Red Lion pub since re-named "Ye Olde Red Lion" is another public house which has seen many changes over the years. Originally it had a beer licence only and became fully licensed to sell spirits, beer wine and tobacco just before the start of World War two. What were once the outbuildings have been incorporated into the main structure and now form a restaurant and games room while the internal layout has been completely altered. It is doubtful if any of the past owners would recognise it. It was owned many years ago by H & G Simonds, Reading brewers and became a freehouse in the 1950's. What is now the car park was once a large though not particularly deep pond called The Folly pond. This had a retaining wall along its boundary with the pub whilst the other sides often flooded into Green Lane and the High Street. Never an attractive feature and usually covered with scum and chickweed, it was filled in during the war. At the rear of the car park stands a thatched building known as the Roundhouse, so called because it was once round. Many years and several extensions later it now hides behind a garage and its former unusual beauty has been lost for ever. .

CHAPTER THIRTY FOUR

From the Red Lion pub, Green Lane takes us through that part of the Village known as Horsemoor, where many picturesque cottages are to be found. Several smaller terraced cottages have been adapted to form one larger property but no other new buildings have been erected for the past twenty five to thirty years. Horsemoor was once the home of a Primitive Methodist Chapel, presumably this was closed when the new Methodist Chapel was built in the High Street in 1914. No trace of this building now remains. Another cottage I well remember was Laurel Cottage in Horsemoor, occupied by my Grandparents. My earliest memories are as a five year old schoolboy walking there each day for my lunch, my mother at that time working full time as a book keeper for Shepherd's Bakery. I recall rows of strongly scented white hyacinths and other spring flowers which grew in front of the cottage, these to be followed in season by masses of lilies, lupins and towering hollyhocks. Gran's cooking on a solid fuel range was always the best ever.there was always a kindly old dog to make a fuss of and also chickens in a run at the end of the garden. As a boy I must have been top heavy as most of the photographs taken with my Grandparents show me with one or both knees swathed in bandages. Boys' knees and gravel paths have very little in common and I still carry the scars to prove it.

Another feature of the garden was a huge hop plant which completely covered the privy and adjoining shed near the back gate. My Grandmother was very hard working, very musical, and an accomplished needlewoman. Before I started school she looked after me while my Mother was at work. Often I would fall over and get in a mess, making mud pies and the like. When my Mother came to collect me at tea time, I would often be arrayed in a smart new linen suit which had been made to replace the soiled one. At the age of seven or eight I can remember my Gran making me a knitted cardigan in pale blue with back panels of a similarly coloured linen material. How I hated that thing, and would ensure that I was last out of the door during school playtime in an effort to keep the garment unseen by my peers.

Laurel cottage had no sink and the only water available was from a well supplied by rain water. This was the only supply until the 1950's when mains water was laid on and consisted of a stand pipe in the garden. The taste of a slice of Shepherd's cottage loaf still warm from the oven and covered in butter was an unbelievable joy. In winter, the butter in the dish was extremely hard and would be held in front of the open fire and warmed to allow it to be spread. Likewise toast made in front of an open wood fire on a home made wire toasting fork bears little or no comparision to today's mass produced bread cooked in an electric toaster.

My Grandfather was an exceptionally kind and understanding man. He had a wonderful singing voice which he exercised regularly in the Methodist Chapel. He also played a cornet. As a boy I would often lead him a merry dance.Once he was about to kill a cockerel for lunch. This must have been some special occasion, chicken being a rare delicacy in those days. Before he arrived home from work, Doug Faithful and myself caught the unfortunate bird and with a single blow from a chopper decapitated it in the wood shed. Talk about 'running round like a headless chicken' this one ran for some fifteen yards before expiring, leaving a trail of blood in its wake. Grandad was not amused.

When I was aged twelve or thirteen, I would sleep overnight at Horsemoor on a Friday night, so that I could be up at five o'clock to go to Church Farm and have the milking cows in before Bob Weaver and the cowman arrived. This involved driving some eighty to ninety cows from their pasture to the cowsheds and tying them up with neck chains. All this carried out for the love of the job.

My Grandparents had a very long and happy life together and celebrated their Diamond wedding receiving a highly prized telegram of congratulations from Her Majesty the Queen. Gran lived to be ninety six.

CHAPTER THIRTY FIVE

At the end of Laurel Cottage garden stand a pair of cottages known as Wood View and Lilac Cottage. The garden of Wood View was on the opposite side of the lane and also housed the 'privy'. This was of the pattern in which the seat was fixed above a large deep hole, the emptying of which was usually an annual occurrence and not a particularly pleasant one. George Phillips and his family lived in this cottage and one moonlit evening the neighbours were aroused by loud cries of distress. The seat of the privy had collapsed leaving George suspended over the hole. Fortuately his cries were heard and he was saved from falling in, otherwise he would certainly have come to a sticky end.

Opposite Laurel Cottage, Lilac Cottage and Woodview stood another pair of cottages, all being occupied by tenants from the landlord W.H. Shepherd. These cottages were offered for sale to the individual tenants at a price in the region of £100 each, my grandfather's cottage Laurel Cottage, being somewhat larger was priced at £180. This vast sum was well beyond the means of any of the tenants and no one was able to take up the offer. Many years later the pair of cottages previously occupied by Slip Leach were and Jockey Hughes were converted to one dwelling by Dr. Nickson when he came to the village.

Radnalls Farm and its cottages stand to the east of Green Lane (BW no. 7), with a further pair of thatched farm cottages at the edge of the old A34 road. This pair of cottages were demolished when the A34 was realigned and a new road from Graces Lane now serves the farm and remaining cottages. One of the farm cottages was home to Nurse Martin (no relation) who was District Nurse to the village, while the next cottage was occupied by Mr. Freddy Colbourn who was pig-man to the Weaver family when a large number of pigs were kept at New Sheds. The last house in Green Lane was built on the site of a pair of cottages occupied by Albert Faithful and family and Horace Leach and family. The new house built on this site named The Studio was the home of Francis Bacon the artist, who lived there for several years. He returned to his more familiar life style in London complaining that this particular spot was "too quiet". He of course had no idea that the M4 and now the new A34 would both come within a stone's throw of the property. Although his meaning 'too quiet' probably did not refer to the noise of the traffic.

Some quarter of a mile south on the A34 towards Newbury stood a house called Hill Cafe on what was a considerably sharp incline on the road, opposite a small wood of mainly oak trees.

This house was owned by Mr. Fulcher who ran a transport cafe and provided overnight accommodation for lorry drivers, this probably being one of the first enterprises of its kind during and immediately after the war. Latterly it became a private house and stood almost in the position occupied by the M4 junction.

Beyond this towards Newbury was a house and three terraced cottages known as Sevenacres. The house, Birds Farm and its adjoining loose boxes was owned by Captain and Mrs. John Glover who operated a riding school and bred pedigree fox terriers which they successfully showed at Crufts. They were responsible for teaching many local residents to ride and having purchased and erected a war-time aeroplane hangar on the site, ran one of the very first indoor riding schools in the area. On his retirement Captain Glover spent every spare moment of his time on the upkeep of Chieveley Church yard whilst Mrs. Glover was the instigator of the Chieveley Evergreen Club for the elderly in the village. On the site of their house and the riding school now stands the Newbury Hilton North Hotel.

Adjacent to the entrance to the Hotel are three cottages. In one of these lived Mrs. Philips and her son Willie who though partially disabled and suffering from epilepsy, regularly made the trip to Church where he pumped the organ before the days of an electrically operated blower. He unfortunately met his end by falling down the well which stood near the entrance to the cottages.

The cottages now provide staff accommodation for the Hilton Hotel. This Hotel has become an island site with the completion. of the new A34/M4 underpass. This major undertaking has been needed for many years to eliminate the existing roundabout which was believed to be the worst bottleneck on the trunk road between the Scotland and Spain. The A34 was originally built as the Preston-Winchester bypass.

CHAPTER THIRTY SIX

From the village end of School Road runs a lane to Horsemoor and Church Farm (Bw's 6a and 7). On a corner site now stands a bungalow. This was an area known as Wests Orchard. This orchard, to the delight of many schoolboys, contained apple and plum trees together with an old thatched summer house which was home to a couple of old black Berkshire sows, who always appeared to have a host of piglets with them,. whilst chicken, ducks and geese had the run of the place. Just beyond this site was a corrugated iron and timber building which had been a sports pavilion in its early life. This housed various farm animals but because of its dilapidated state eventually collapsed. Church Farm had a pair of cowmen's cottages, now one house. The farm was an array of cowsheds, barns and a dairy run by the Weaver family of Braziers Farm. John Weaver ran the arable side and Bob Weaver looked after the dairy. This was a very pleasant spot in the summer. Wild flowers abounded, and stinging nettles, while high hawthorn hedges covered in blossoms and later with rosy red berries lined the track towards Spring Gardens, Chieveley fields and New Sheds (FP no. 5). Winter however took on a more solemn and sombre tone when the whole area became a sea of mud, being churned twice daily by the feet of some hundred or so dairy cows making their way to and from their grazing to the cowsheds for milking, also by the many horses and carts carrying swedes, mangolds and hay and often frozen loads of kale to feed the cattle. The hay, prior to the advent of the automatic baler was made in the fields and built into ricks. Then in winter, cut into trusses using a deadly looking device called a hay knife, a blade of some 30 inches long by 6 inches wide tapering to a point at one end, with a T-shaped handle some 18 inches long set at the wide end of the blade. Grasping the handle with both hands, the point of the blade was then driven into the rick cutting the hay into blocks which were then tied with binder twine, before being carted to where it was required. This was a very labour intensive and often dangerous occupation.

Between the hawthorn lined track to New Sheds and Green Lane ran another similar track known as Donkey Lane (Bw 7), still in existence but without the hedges. On the village side of Donkey lane was Spring Gardens which consisted of some twenty or so allotments. Very few of these were cultivated in my time, probably because of the start of the war and the fact that there was no water close by. During the war when the "Dig for Victory" campaign was launched the school took on two plots and a group of the older boys (ages 12 to 13) armed with garden forks and spades started to remove the couch grass and other weeds from the site prior to planting potatoes. The clearance resulted in a pile of rubbish at one plot and was formed into the shape of a large nest and became known as the "eagles nest" capable of accommodating several boys. However less and less time was given to digging and more and more time spent in the aforementioned "nest" smoking many packets of Mrs. Hammond's Woodbines or if anyone had the extra penny we would lash out and buy a packet of "Black Cat". These were always followed by a bag of aniseed balls to disguise the smell of tobacco. During the whole of the summers I cannot remember being caught smoking by the Headmaster who made an occasional visit to Spring Gardens. Neither can I recall ever digging a crop of potatoes.

Country boys had and I hope still have, a wide knowledge of the local flora and fauna especially where trees were concerned. Any large tree was approached in the same way that a mountaineer views a mountain. Because it is there it has to be climbed and this was something at which most lads of my age seemed to be particular adept, especially at birdnesting time. Rooks regularly built their large untidy nests at the top of elm trees until most of these trees succumbed to Dutch elm disease.

A row of elm trees stood at the rear of the Churchyard shed, the topmost branches of which provided excellent nesting for many pairs of rooks. One cold, wet and windy March day, the writer, having been dared, climbed to the top of one of these trees to collect rooks' eggs, a hazardous occupation but a boy of twelve is not to be deterred especially in front of his school mates. Having found a nest containing eggs the next priority is deciding how to get them safely to the ground. In those days we had an option not available to boys of today in that we all wore peaked caps. This being so, the eggs were placed inside the peak of the cap and brought down to earth. Unfortunately on this day the cap was laid on the ground still containing the eggs, when someone, and as I recall it was Brian Bosley accidentally stepped on it. Five rooks' eggs make a fair omelette in a cap and called for a lot of explanation when I returned home, being afraid to admit that I had been forty or more feet up a tree to collect the eggs.

Recently when varnishing the church door in mid April, I listened to the familiar noise of young rooks calling for food. This reminded me of my climb for eggs one day in March long ago. The tree that I climbed is still there and is not an elm tree at all.but is in fact a sycamore which is now much larger and covered in ivy, the elms having succumbed to Dutch Elm disease in the 1960's. This year the sycamore has no rooks nests in it, although there are several in the adjoining trees. I can only assume that generations of rooks have warned their successors about the demon egg stealer who raided their nests more than sixty years ago. Little do they realise that they have nothing to fear from this particular quarter any longer.

CHAPTER THIRTY SEVEN

SCHOOLBOYS, AND THERE were always some of us hanging around at Church Farm, were always in demand when cattle needed moving from one site to another, especially if this entailed their being driven through the village. Cattle have little or no sense of direction and when being moved up or down the High Street were always intent on entering any garden with an open gate. It was the duty of the herders to get in front of the herd and endeavour, with much waving of arms and shouting, to keep them to the intended route. Many years later after moving into Corner House a herd of some twenty cattle belonging to Mr. Basil Povey decided to take a short cut across a newly sown lawn during a very wet spell. I well recall using such phrases as 'Oh dear' and words to that effect. Also at that time, I owned three bullocks who broke down the fence between their paddock and the lawn of Marymead where they ran amok, taking me some two days to repair the damage.

Michael Pocock remembers as a lad helping to drive a herd of heifers from New Farm to Downend. This was for the owner Mr. Basil Povey who promised to pay the sum of one shilling for this service. He does not remember much about the actual drive, but recalls the fact that he is still owed the shilling.

CHAPTER THIRTY EIGHT

A SEASONAL SPORT WAS that of rabbiting. Before the coming of the combine harvester, corn was cut with a mechanical binder which cut the corn and tied it into sheaves which were then ejected and laid in rows around the field, eventually to be picked up by hand and put into "stooks" or "shocks" to dry, prior to collection again by hand when they were pitched onto carts and taken away to be built into ricks. These ricks were built in a rickyard at the farm or in a corner of the field where the crop had been grown. The ricks were thatched with straw to keep out the weather and stood there until the following Spring or Summer. They were built just far enough apart to allow a threshing machine to be positioned between them and then the work of threshing began. Quite a large team of men would be involved, usually two pitchers on the rick, one man on top of the machine feeding the corn into the drum, another at the rear of the threshing machine bagging up the corn and loading it onto a wagon. This was no mean feat as a "West of England" sack full of wheat weighed two and one quarter hundredweight, barley being easier to manage at only two hundredweight. Another man would be dealing with the straw which was usually fed into an elevator and built into another rick, to be used as cattle feed and bedding. Also, the better quality straw would be set aside for thatching the roofs of farm cottages and buildings. Another by-product was wheat chaff which was saved to be mixed with oats and formed the main feed for cart horses. Before mechanisation as much as twenty per cent of the arable land on a farm was given over to the production of oats purely to feed the cart horses. Local boys had great fun at threshing time, for as the ricks had stood for some time, they had attracted large colonies of rats and mice who had taken advantage of the warm dry conditions and abundance of food. At threshing time a fence of netting wire was erected round the rick to prevent rats escaping. This afforded the local lads, together with the occasional terrier, much enjoyment chasing the vermin with sticks and disposing of as many as possible. Often the tally from a single rick would be one hundred or more rats and mice. Most farms had a large population of vermin which seemed to survive despite the numerous half-wild cats which roamed the yards and buildings.

The power to drive the threshing tackle was originally supplied by a large steam driven traction engine, but in later years tractors were adapted with a belt drive pulley wheel and this method took over from the larger machines. The site of this operation was a noisy and very dangerous place to be, with many unguarded pulley belts and wheels. The whole business of threshing finally ended with the coming of the combine harvester, enabling the farmer to harvest the crop direct from the field.

When the remaining crop was being cut, the standing corn area diminished in size, so the population of wild rabbits moved inwards. They would then squat just inside the edge of the standing corn awaiting the time to make a bolt for freedom. They were then stalked by the avid hunter, armed with a stout stick. If a rabbit made a dash for it the stubble and the sheaves on the ground made it difficult for the animal to escape, especially when chased by a gang of men and boys all yelling at the top of their voices. The rabbits stood little chance of escape. Many a proud hunter would return home laden with the spoils of the day which made a welcome addition to the family diet.

After the harvest had been gathered and ricked the farmer would allow villagers who kept their own poultry to go and glean, which entailed gathering the ears of corn which had fallen during the cutting process. These would be collected by many local housewives and carted home in old prams or other suitable conveyances to provide winter feed for their domestic fowl.

Another task undertaken by the housewife was that of gathering wood for fuel to heat the water in their coppers, both for washing clothes and bathing, these operations usually being carried out on a weekly basis. It was not an unusual sight to see five or six ladies returning from Bussock Wood with their old prams loaded to capacity. The collection of this wood was allowed by the owner, at that time Mr. Vincent, on the condition that no axes or saws were used. Consequently the wood collected was dry and rotten, ideally suited for the copper hole which had an enormous appetite and would take only a couple of wash days to consume a complete pram load of wood.

CHAPTER THIRTY NINE

New Sheds was a brick building which lay between Church Farm and Bussock Wood. It had an enclosed yard where Freddy Colbourn single handedly looked after Weaver's pigs which was a very lonely job and a large flock of free range hens. During the summer months these birds would not return to their chicken houses until late in the evening. As Freddy had gone home by this time, it was the job of Bob Weaver, usually accompanied by his retinue of schoolboys, to make the journey from Church Farm to New Sheds to shut the hens up for the night.

One night the pop-hole door of one house had not been correctly shut and a fox managed to get into the house. The scene of devastation the next morning cannot adequately be described. There were some forty or fifty hens all lying dead ,most of which had their heads bitten off, and not a single bird appeared to have been injured in any other way.

Another memory I have was on a very dark night, when riding a trade bicycle along a cattle track across the fields from New Sheds back to the farm. Travelling at quite a fast pace and with no lights I ran into a one of a herd of milking cows in the field. This poor creature was lying across the path and was probably just as surprised as I at this sudden coming together. No damage was done apart from a few grazes and a new front wheel needed for the trade bike, this work being carried out by Mr. Thomas at the Red Lion the next day. I never knew the identity of the offending cow as it disappeared into the darkness after having been so rudely awakened.

Another similar exploit took place on the same machine on another pitch dark night. Bob Weaver had gone into Braziers Farm at the East Lane entrance, leaving me to ride the bicycle round to the front entrance in the High Street. At the junction I came into contact with a solid object. A strong hand gripped my shoulder and a bright torch shone in my face. To my horror I discovered that I had run into our local Special Constable. I was dragged into Braziers Farm where he got into heated discussion with Bob Weaver. They must have resolved the matter amicably as I heard no more of the incident, having cleared off home while the argument was taking place. It may appear irresponsible, however no one to my recollection ever had a bicycle with a light on it, until such time as we lads started work which involved cycling to Newbury each day. A light was invaluable when one had to turn a bicycle upside down and repair a puncture at the roadside, sometimes in the dark and rain.

CHAPTER FORTY

SEVERAL YEARS BEFORE the war, Charlie Belcher and his family had
lived at New Sheds which at that time was called Belcher's Palace.
Sadly no trace of this now remains or of the pond which adjoined it
providing the only source of water.

The allotments at spring Gardens fell into decline and with the
removal of the boundary fence the whole area became general arable
land. After wasting many hours on the allotment in the run up to
the summer holidays, on their return to school, most of the older
boys were employed by the local farmers, picking up potatoes. For
this they were paid the princely sum of three and a half pence an
hour, with the exception of a farmer at Winterbourne, Mr. Palmer,
who raised the hourly rate to four pence just under two and half
new pence, but to earn this magnificent sum, the boys had to cycle
to Boxford Common and also provide their own buckets. The work
usually started about eight in the morning until five in the evening,
with a break at mid-day. At this time a fire would be lighted and
the biggest potatoes found in the morning placed in the embers to
bake. Needless to say these were never cooked thoroughly but young
digestive systems seemed to cope with this diet. A drink was a bottle
of water brought from home. In most cases, the potato spinner, a

device for removing the potatoes from the ground, was drawn by a tractor with the exception of North Heath Farm, owned by Mr. Baylis, where the potatoes were grown on the Common and the spinner being drawn by horses under the control of the head carter, Mr. Sprules. This machine was pulled along the crop, one row at a time, and the potatoes thrown by the claws of the spinner into rows. Each boy then had his own stretch to pick up before the spinner returned on its next trip. Full buckets were then emptied into sacks which had been placed at the end of the rows. Hard work for thirteen year- olds but stood them in good stead for even harder work later in life. At the end of the day each picker took home in his lunch bag one or two of the largest potatoes he had found during the day to be cooked properly, plus his wages - approximately two shillings and eight pence, or in today's money less than fifteen pence for a full days hard graft.

CHAPTER FORTY ONE

CHURCH FARM WAS used in the making of a war time film which showed the difference between the old fashioned method of milking cows by hand and the new way, using a milking machine in a purpose built milking parlour. Church farm was used as the old fashioned example and the milking parlour filmed at another location. Intense rivalry developed between the local boys to drive cows out of the milking sheds in an attempt to be caught on film. I don't think any of us ever made it and if we did no one saw the finished film anyway. Eventually one of the barns was turned into a milking parlour with a state-of- the- art milking machine and much of the magic of past times was lost for ever. Church farm has seen many changes since then and what was the milking parlour is now a private home.

The coming of the milking machine drastically altered the way of life on the dairy farm. The first type of machine was an individual vacuum operated device fitted with a milking unit and carried to each cow in turn. When the milk container was full (two to three gallons) it had to be carried manually to the dairy where a large refrigerated storage container held the day's yield prior to its collection by a tanker lorry owned by what was then the Milk Marketing Board. After this the milking parlour was introduced and cows were driven into each of the bays (Church Farm unit having six bays) to be milked. During this time each cow was automatically fed an allotted amount of concentrated food. The milk was then pumped directly from this unit to the main storage tank in the dairy.

All the above was a very far cry from the manual method of milking. In the old fashioned way all the cows entered the cow shed and were tethered by a neck chain, each having its own individual place. A manger ran the full length of the building and food would be placed in it before the cows entered. It required several people to milk a herd of some eighty to one hundred cows, this taking place twice daily and during the winter months both taking place in darkness, one commencing at about five o'clock in the morning and the next session at between four and five in the afternoon. All this was carried out by the light of hurricane lamps before electricity was laid on to the farm buildings in the late 1930's. The milking was done manually by a person who sat on a three legged stool with a milking pail (a semi-covered bucket) held between their knees. Most milkers wore some sort of head covering which was very greasy having been in contact with the side of the cow. Often a cow would object to being milked which resulted in having to have its rear legs tied together with a cord to prevent injury to the milker. Cows unlike horses are capable of kicking forwards as well as backwards. Another ploy often adopted was to tie the cow's tail to one of its back legs. A swishing cow's tail being very unwelcome if in contact with the milker's face or body, especially when the tail was soaking wet, freezing cold and plastered in mud or worse. Another hazardous occupation was passing at the rear of a row of tethered cows particularly in the spring when the green grass had an amazing effect on their digestive systems. The grass which was ingested at the front end of the cow gained in velocity during its passage through the animal and returned to daylight at an alarming rate.

Milk from the dairy at this time was cooled and placed in ten gallon churns. These were then taken to the top of Church Farm lane where they were collected daily by lorry and taken to the local distribution centre in Newbury, called Newbury Creamery and owned by the Goode family.

Most of the local milking herds in the early years would have consisted almost entirely of dairy Short-horn cows with the exception of Captain and Mrs. Wauds' herd of pedigree Guernseys at Bradley Court, many of these were exhibited with great succes at agricultural shows all over the country. After the war the now familiar black and white Friesian became more popular and it is a rare sight today to see any other breed of dairy cow. Indeed with the introduction of the milk quota scheme and continuing restrictions being placed on the dairy farmer, the village now has Fir Tree Farm as its only dairy herd.

Milk for the village produced at Church Farm was delivered round the village outskirts and North Heath by an old Bedford van. This had running boards along each side which were adorned with several school boys during the school holidays,. These boys were very useful making milk deliveries to the various houses. At one stage a pony and trap was used to deliver milk to parts of the village, this often driven by myself during school holidays and on Saturdays, while the rest of the inhabitants were served by Miss Eva Dobson, a relative of the Weavers who lived with them at Braziers Farm. The milk would be brought from Church Farm to Braziers and from there she would carry two two-gallon cans with half pint and pint measures hanging from the handles. With these the milk would be delivered from the can directly to the householders' jug.

I cannot remember her ever complaining even in the worst of weathers and she was always arrayed in rubber boots, a khaki coloured warehouse coat and with a blue beret on her head. Woollen mittens were occasionally seen but usually only in the most severe weather.

Several of us lads aged about twelve or thirteen spent most of our time at Church Farm and I remember a particularly friendly heifer which I would feed and make a special fuss of. Eventually this animal became so tame that I made a halter from binder twine and would ride her round the farm and adjoining meadows. An incident which caused Freddy Colbourne to complain was when we made binder twine harness for young pigs and attached them to old milk churns, and released them to see which would win the race from Church Farm back to New Sheds.

Also at Church Farm was a large, very unfriendly roan coloured shorthorn bull. He was lying full length in the field one day, apparently dead. Pleased to have this notorious creature at our mercy at last, we rushed up and attempted to jump on his inert body. At this point he leapt to his feet, snorting wildly and the assembled company came very close to olympic speeds when exiting the field.

CHAPTER FORTY TWO

RETURNING TO THE village from Church Farm is a large house on the right hand side now called Horsemoor House. This has been the home of several well known local families over the years, some of whose names appear on headstones in the Churchyard including those of Piggott, Muller, and Rayner. .

Turning into School road and going in a westerly direction a telephone sub-station stands on the left hand side. This site is part of a fir plantation which was planted immediately after the end of the war by the owners of the land at that time. This planting effectively prevented any further development of the plot. Before this took place it had been generally assumed that this area would be suitable for development by the local council, being close to the school and village amenities. The council subsequently built houses at Downend called Bardown. This in turn was increased in size some twenty years later. Sadly this second phase of Bardown which included bungalows and three pairs of semi-detached houses are now all empty and awaiting demolition. Quite a sad thought as I personally carried out the plumbing work to all these dwellings when they were first constructed.

Opposite the plantation is the entrance to Sowbury Park an estate of some eighteen houses built in the 1970's on what was New Farm. New Farm consisted of a large thatched barn several outbuildings and a brick built piggery. This was farmed by Mr. Ireland who lived in one of the two farm cottages which have since been converted to one dwelling.. He ran a small mixed farm on land which is now Sowbury Park and the later development of Heathfields.

After losing their ground at Priors Court, Chieveley Cricket Club played in the paddock which is now Sowbury Park. Much work was carried out on this piece of land and a pitch of very high standard was attained and used for several years. Sowbury Path is a footpath which runs from School Road to the Church and was used by children going to and from school. Very few had bicycles and there was no bus service or parents with a car to supply the necessary transport. Many of the children walked as much as two or three miles to school each day and those from the north end of the village used Sowbury Path as a short cut to school. The entrance to the area known as Heathfields was originally part of Mr. Ireland's garden and boasted the finest walnut tree in the village, still in the garden of the first house. Also between this tree and the entrance to the school was a row of cob nut trees. These were always loaded with nuts each autumn, very few of which were ever left for the squirrels. Another hazel nut tree stood in the headmaster's garden and was usually loaded with nuts. This tree overhung the boys' playground and the crop was never touched during school time. Some of these delicious nuts however, were occasionally tasted out of school hours if we had seen Mr. and Mrs. Tanner drive off in their car.

CHAPTER FORTY THREE

OPPOSITE HEATHFIELDS STANDS the old Memorial hall, now very dilapidated. This building was an ex-army construction from the 1st world war and was erected as a memorial in the 1920's by Mr. Rayner of the Manor, to those who served in that war . Many functions were held there, my parents' wedding reception in 1928, dances, whist drives etc. It was home to a Men's club with a billiard room and during the second world war was used by the newly formed Chieveley Boys' Club, the billiard table being a special attraction. Table tennis and boxing were also popular. One of the highlights of the Boys' Club were the evenings with Bob Weaver who played all of the pop songs of the day on the piano together with other old favourites . In later years the billiard table was taken to Arlington Manor for use by the students there when it became the Mary Hare Grammar School.

Our Boys' Club was fortunate in having a very good organiser named Mr. Comber who came to Chieveley most Saturday evenings. He was at that time in charge of Newbury Boys' Club which was situated in Northbrook Street in what had been the Liberal Club and is now a building occupied by a wine-bar.

In 1942/3 the Memorial hall was turned into a dining room and a school meals service was implemented with the meals being supplied from Thatcham. Later the billiard room was turned into a kitchen to cook lunches for the children. Mrs. Booker was cook there for many years and with her several helpers provided excellent meals.

Dances were still held in the Hall in the evenings while the premises were still used as school classrooms in the daytime. Two large white fireclay sinks stood at the edge of the stage filled with water and contained plants, frogs, newts and goldfish. One evening after a session at the Red Lion, several of the locals had eventually arrived at the dance in a high state of inebriation having consumed a new beverage brewed by Messrs. Whitbreads. This was called 'Final Selection' and was a strong barley wine. On the base of the bottle was a small label which read 'Due to the high alcoholic content of this beverage,discretion should be used in it's consumption'. This warning however, not being heeded led to bets being laid as to the number of goldfish that could be consumed whole. As I recall there was no outright winner but no doubt a few upsets stomachs the following morning.

With the building of the new Recreation Centre, the old Memorial Hall was sold and for a short time became Chieveley's one and only Night Club, called appropriately "Tin Lizzy". This however did not last very long. .Since then it has had several changes of ownership ,its last function being that of a domestic appliance repair shop.

CHAPTER FORTY FOUR

ADJOINING THE OLD Hall is a paddock known affectionately as "The Rec" formerly used as a playing field for the school. This land was again donated to the village by Mr. Rayner in return for permission to re-route a footpath which originally ran through the Manor garden. In the early years, "Camp" meetings were held in the paddock on Sunday afternoons with the preacher speaking from the bed of a large Berkshire farm waggon. The meetings were usually well attended, popular hymns being sung to the accompaniment of a visiting Silver or Brass band, Chieveley never having had a band of its own. Refreshments were provided by the organisers, the whole affair taking on the air of a large picnic, the success of the afternoon being dependant on the weather. .

These events were a favourite meeting place for the young people. During the summer most of the young men would be employed on the land for six days a week and many of the girls who were in service would have just a half day off on a Sunday. Dances were few and young ladies seldom if ever visited a public house on their own so the opportunities to meet the opposite sex were few and far between. No doubt many a romance was begun following a "camp" meeting,. it often being the only time young people had occasion to meet someone of their own age from a neighbouring village, this being in the days when public transport was in its infancy. The only other means of travel was on foot or bicycle.

The "Rec" was also visited annually by a small circus which was always very popular. The Cricket Club played on this ground for some two or three seasons before the preparation of a wicket at the new Recreation Centre. It proved to be rather small for cricket, due partly to the row of horse-chestnut trees which bordered the paddock on the road side. These trees although a hindrance to the cricketers did however, provide conkers to many generations of Chieveley children. This age-old children's sport now appears to be under threat in some parts of the country as the powers that be deem it to be a dangerous and hazardous occupation one council even contemplating cutting down the horse chestnut trees as a safety measure. One wonders what sort of crackpot schemes they will dream up next.

In a far corner of the paddock was a large pit with sloping grassed sides which provided us with the only incline in the village for sledges when there was snow, which then seemed to fall every winter. One particularly popular sledge that we used was a pony-sled with a seat for two passengers and a board at the back on which the driver stood. This belonged to the Reverend Hazel and he had brought it home with him from Canada. Having no pony we would haul it manually but nevertheless had great times with it. The pit has since been filled in. When the M4 motorway was constructed the "Rec" provided the site for road builders' caravans, but has now been returned as grazing for horses.

Mr. George Shepherd (Shop Owner) with Fred Leach
(Grandfather and baker) and Henry John Leach (Roundsman)

Chieveley High Street facing south from Church Corner.

Prismalls' shop and bakery. The Chalet and the Crooked House.

Chieveley High Street facing North from Church Corner showing the Maypole with the Crooked House in the distance.

Chieveley High Street south showing old Infant School and Hammonds sweet shop.

The Wheatsheaf public house and The Mount

Coombe House, Chieveley High Street

Chieveley Manor

*The Hare & Hounds public house and cottages (Quality Court) in
East Lane*

Great Grandad Barrett

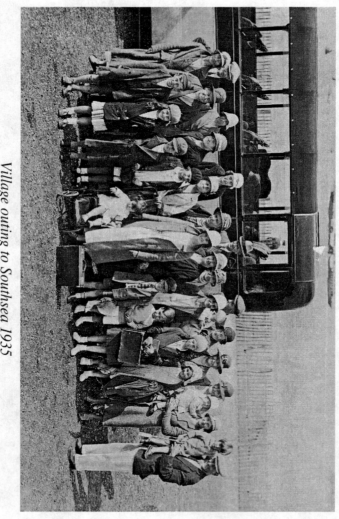

Village outing to Southsea 1935

Jack Martin (Writer's father) being presented with his medal by
H.M. Queen Mary at the Army Cup final 1920.

CHAPTER FORTY FIVE

OPPOSITE THE REC stands the School which dates from 1898 and was segregated into boys and girls although the sexes were mixed in class. Tuition was for children between the ages of 5 and 14 and divided into four classes. The school day was from 9 am to 3.45 pm with a lunch break of one hour. Before the advent of school meals, most children would make the journey home while those who lived too far away, provided their own sandwiches. Free milk was supplied each morning this being a third of a pint bottle, a drinking straw being inserted through a hole in the cardboard stopper. As I recall, the cane was also readily available. One Headmaster, Mr. Gurth Hale, lost a relation on the Titanic. During my school days the Headmaster was Mr Victor Tanner, who lived with his wife and son Patrick in the adjoining School House. Miss Morgan and Miss Hazel taught the infants, Mrs. Holmes the intermediate class and the Headmaster taught the older pupils. After my time at school Mr. Tanner was joined by a Deputy Head, Mr. Basham, who despite their names were very good teachers. Mr. Tanner did not use the cane very often but when he did the recipient was left in agony for several hours. My hands still tingle after all these years when I recall that cane. Another though less severe punishment would be meted out as he walked up behind an unattentive pupil sitting at a desk. He would catch the offender a smart flick on the ear with his quite large signet ring. This had the effect of trapping ones ear against the side of the head and could be very painful indeed. The school became a Primary school in the 1950's when the leaving age was increased and the older children went on to the Kennet School in Thatcham. They now go from Chieveley to The Downs School at Compton. Since my day the school has been greatly enlarged with the addition of classrooms, a kitchen and a hall together with a new playing field at the rear of the building,also a new heating system, a far cry from the old coke fired boiler which stood in the Classroom of Standard Two, surrounded by buckets of coke to be fed into the boiler as required, by the older boys.

Life at school in the mid thirties was quite hard affair. Almost all the pupils arriving on foot, some having walked considerable distances,. often the last few hundred yards at a vastly increased pace when the bell started to ring. This usually started to ring at five minutes to nine and those not inside by the appointed time at nine o clock really had to have a good excuse for being late, or suffer the consequences which entailed being given lines to write, being kept in after school or the cane which was reserved for persistent offenders. After our mid morning bottle of milk there followed a frantic rush to get outside into the playground. This of course was segregated into boys one side of the fence and girls the other. "Treat" days were looked forward to particularly the Christmas party held in the Memorial hall opposite. After an excellent tea of sandwiches and cakes each child was given an orange and a small bag of sweets and all departed for home in the dark feeling on top of the world except for those few who had over indulged on the goodies. If only the youngsters of today could be as easily satisfied.

Sports days and prize giving were happy times but less enjoyable were the regular visits of the School Nurse whose main task seemed to be the detection and destruction of head lice. The worst dread of any pupil at the school was the annual visit of the School Dentist, who apparently delighted in filling or "stopping" as then called, as many teeth as possible. I can recall no anaesthetic ever being used but will never forget the foot operated treadle machine with its large driving wheel and many pulleys and belts which in turn drove the dreaded drill. These times are now referred to as "the good old days". Debatable I think. Throughout the school year points were awarded for good work and added to those gained on sports day to determine the winner of the House Cup. The school was divided into four 'Houses', these being Palmer, Vincent, Fairhurst and Rayner, named after the owners of the four major properties in the area. They were most probably members of the school Board of Governors and who had provided the most coveted House Cup. This cup was presented on Prize Giving Day and spent its time prominently displayed in a glass case on a shelf above the Headmaster's desk in the main class room.

Boys started school wearing short trousers and made the transition to long ones at about the age of thirteen . At age fourteen our schooling ended and we started work . No type of uniform existed apart from a grey school cap for the boys sporting a badge with the letters "CCS" (Chieveley Council School). In the early 60's when my own children attended the school, both boys and girls wore grey uniforms with green ties for the boys and socks with green tops. During my time at school, I well remember many a child attracting the attention of the teacher "please sir I en't got no ink" to be corrected 'please sir I have no ink'. This usually entailed the trip to the Headmaster's office, always known as the Private Room, to collect a white enamel jug with a spout. This jug contained ink and was used to replenish the ink wells which were fitted at both ends of the school desks. These desks seated two boys or girls, never mixed, each desk lid tipped up as did the seats, the latter being the most uncomfortable seats imaginable.

The school day started with assembly and roll-call - some ninety to one hundred pupils in all, then prayers followed by a hymn. Tuition took the form of the three R's, with geography, history and the occasional spelling bee. Physical recreation or 'games' took place on a Wednesday afternoon in the Rec. Football for the boys was played during the winter months but was dependent on the school's only football not being punctured. Our goalposts consisted of four poles cut in Bussock Wood with no crossbars or nets. During the summer term cricket was played by the boys but with very primitive equipment while the girls occupied their time with stool-ball and rounders.

How quickly times change, only four years after leaving school at fourteen, I happened to be home on leave from the army, and passing the Rec on a sports day an amazing transformation had taken place. The school team were now resplendant in green and white 'strip', the pitch marked out and new goal posts with nets. Also some six or more new footballs. The coaching was being carried out by J. Macbride who was currently the goal keeper for Reading Football Club.

There were no foreign language lessons, however, Mr. Tanner the headmaster would occasionally read to a class and I remember enjoying "Les Miserables". Many varied tasks fell to the older boys, those of thirteen years, such as carrying in the crates of milk, stoking the boiler and digging and weeding the school flower gardens. I cannot remember ever having been given homework to do or receiving any sex education. As most children spent time at one farm or another their knowledge of the subject was quite extensive and was helped considerably by following, in the twilight hours, the antics of the local Land Army girls and their American military escorts. No school journeys were made to Newbury to enjoy the swimming baths, or any other particular outing. This however, was probably because of the severe fuel restrictions in force at the time.

It was impossible to forecast that any of us would live to see calculators, computers and the like in common use in the school classroom. . Indeed television was not available and at its inception, was for many years restricted to one channel in black and white. The early models had a screen 9" wide (23cm) and the programmes commenced early evening and ran for a few hours before closing down. Television news and programme presenters wore evening dress for any programmes scheduled for 6 pm and after. The National Anthem was always played at the close of transmission.

During the winter or if the weather was wet, playtimes were spent in the appropriately named "boys' and girls' sheds". These were open sided sheds, one in each playground, measuring some 20 x 60 feet in size with a corrugated iron roof, fresh air and exercise being the order of the day.

Also at the top end of the playground stood the toilets, a row of four cubicles with wooden seats above galvanized buckets for use by the girls with one similar cubicle and a brick wall painted black over a trough for use as a urinal for the boys, this latter being open to all weathers. In snow or heavy rain the trip to the toilets could in no way be deemed an enjoyable experience.

CHAPTER FORTY SIX

THE COMING OF the second world war brought many changes, not only to our lives but also to the school. The influx of evacuees almost doubled the number of pupils overnight. These "townies" seemed to us to be a know-all crowd and it was some time before any sort of integration took place,this not being achieved until after a considerable number scuffles and some minor blood-letting. After some weeks most of us became firm friends and some of the families have stayed on in the village and have now been accepted as 'locals', one such being Harry Argent who has just completed his fifty years acceptance period and can now officially be called a 'Chieveleyite'.

Initially we were amazed to find that many of the evacuees had never seen a cow or knew how milk was produced. They were probably equally surprised at the primitive toilet facilities which most cottages had. A story most often told was of the evacuee who complained to his host that there was no bolt on the privy door, only to be advised that 'in the last fifty years no one had ever tried to steal the bucket'. It would be fairly true to say that we resented some of their 'know-all' ways and would often set traps for them. One such was during the autumn when fallen leaves littered the road sides. These we would make into inviting piles for them to kick. Sometimes a pile of leaves would conceal a large stone or brick causing many a sore toe.

Over the past ten years or so, the last Friday evening in September is given over to a reunion of 'old Chieveley boys', this takes place at the Fox and Hounds, Arlington. Many of the older members reminisce over their pints and discuss the happenings of yesteryear.

To my knowledge no boy or girl from Chieveley School has ever made their name as Prime Minister, or achieved any other exalted position.

CHAPTER FORTY SEVEN

AT THE FOOT of the hill past the school lies the 'Ford', so named for it was originally just that. Correctly it should be called the Winter Bourne. Legend has it that this stream only ran once every seven years,. the flow being generated by springs rising beyond Hazelhanger about a mile to the west. However, I recall the stream running on several consecutive years. The flow has been more constant since the 1980's when a pumping station was installed at the site of the gravel pits and the source of the springs, and an 18" diameter pipe now carries a supply from there to the river Lambourn at Bagnor, this being part of a grand scheme to supply additional water to the Thames. This scheme also prevents flooding in the 'long meadow' between Grove Road (FP 38) and Hazelhanger farm. This flooding took place most summers when the springs were at their height. As boys, many hours were spent 'swimming' in the Ford, especially when an impromptu dam was built to increase the depth of water which never exceeded 24 inches. Another 'dare' was to crawl under the culvert at the lower end of Grove road, a distance of some ten to twelve feet, when the water was running, leaving only a few inches of head room to allow the intrepid boy to breathe. This was an extremely stupid act which in later years my own children were told never to attempt.

On either side of the road near the ford stood several very large elm trees with farm buildings on the south side of the road, the site nearer to the road now being used as a sewerage works. In the ford beyond Hazelhanger grew some excellent watercress, which we often gathered after removing boots and socks. The water was usually icy cold as the crop is only recognised as fit for human consumption when there is an R in the month.

Almost a mile beyond the School lies North Heath. Prior to the building of the current school village children could probably recall the exact distance in paces as they had to make this journey on foot to attend the school held in what is now the garage of the North Heath house. This school was built in 1839 and became a National School in about 1854 and taught some one hundred children from the age of seven years. The school continued to operate until after the opening of the Infant School in the High Street and appears to have closed towards the end of the 1800's.

Although now mainly enclosed, the common was in those days an open space only coming into cultivation in the early years of the second world war. Continuing straight ahead from the school road towards the west, a track runs towards the Blue Boar, now called the Crab. To the left of this track stood a row of enormous elm trees, now long disappeared having fallen victim to Dutch elm disease, a scourge which accounted for the demise of many such wonderful trees which were so plentiful in this part of the country. At the time when most of these magnificent trees met their end, a good supply of firewood became available, and domestic wood burning appliances became popular but now like the trees themselves, are seldom seen.

Rooks also suffered dramatically as these large elms provided an ideal situation for nesting,. many dozens of breeding pairs often building in the same tree. Due to their early pairing off and nest building usually February/March these nest were very conspicuous having been built and occupied long before the host tree came into leaf. These rookeries as they were known became a very noisy affair especially when the young birds hatched and required feeding.

CHAPTER FORTY EIGHT

THE TRACK ACROSS the common joins up with the Newbury/Wantage road and at this junction stands the Blue Boar pub. This has been known as such since the early sixteen hundreds and boasts a figure of a Blue Boar which stands on a plinth at the south east corner of the building. This statue was removed from Ripley Castle in Yorkshire by the troops of Oliver Cromwell on the eve of the Battle of Marston Moor, which took place in July 1644. On one occasion in the 1950's it was stolen but recovered after a few weeks and has remained in its existing position ever since. Cromwell's army is reported to have camped at North Heath in October 1644 prior to the Battle of Newbury, and their Commander allegedly spent the night at the pub. Another long held belief was that a tunnel existed between the Blue Boar and Hop Castle, a folly building some distance to the west. Having examined the cellar of the Blue Boar no trace of any such tunnel is visible.

The first landlord I can recall at this pub was Pop Saville who was there until the early 1950's. This was before electricity was available, the only light being from oil lamps. To enable the game of darts to be played a piece of shiny tin was bent at right angles and placed behind the oil lamp to shed additional light on the dart board. Another feature was a strip of plaster gouged out of the ceiling between the throwing point or oche and the dart board. This was because the ceiling being very low, was struck by darts when attempting to go for numbers at the top of the board.

The next Landlord/owner was Mr Ernie Cox who ran the business with his wife Elsie, they both having come to Chieveley from Wales. He was reputed to have purchased the pub and adjoining land from Messrs. H & G Simmons the brewers (now Courage) for the sum of £3,000. Some years later the pub was bought by Mr. John Booth, whose family still farm at Penclose farm, and under his ownership became one of the first public houses in the district to open a restaurant. This proved to be extremely popular, so much so that there are few public houses today which do not offer a similar facility. Over the last twenty years the Blue Boar has changed hands on several occasions, each new owner carrying out alterations, none so much as the present owner who is reported to have spent vast sums of money adding accommodation and other facilities. Today's prices, when a pint of beer can exceed £2.50 are a far cry from the early days when I remember a pint of mild and bitter, a bag of Smith's crisps with the salt in the blue screw of paper and a saucer of pickled onions could be purchased for less than a shilling or five new pence.

CHAPTER FORTY NINE

NEARBY LIES NORTH Heath Farm which has been owned and farmed by the Baylis family for many years., together with Winterbourne Farm. Mr. & Mrs. John Baylis still live in North Heath farmhouse, but many if not all of the adjoining farm cottages are now privately owned, most being two or more cottages knocked into one, to form a larger house.

These homes are now occupied by two or three residents where previously the smaller cottages were often home to a family of as many as ten or more. Of the two cottages one was occupied by Bill Smith and his wife, hence the name Smith's cottage. Bill was a loyal member of the Chieveley branch of the Royal British Legion and for many years proudly carried the banner for the annual Armistice Day parade at Chieveley War Memorial. Next door lived Les Holmes with his wife and family, Bill, Mary, Alec, Peter, Ted and Annie. They may have lost some children prior to Alec's birth as he was the third eldest but had the unusual second Christian name of Sevenus (7). He and I shared a desk as school and played football together for Chieveley Minors. Regrettably he lost his life just before his seventeen birthday in a drowning accident at the gravel pits.

In the days when milk and groceries were delivered by Weavers and Shepherds, a track ran along the front of the cottages on the north east side of the common. This has now been fenced off and the gardens extended out to the road.

From North Heath common Old Street (BW no. 12) runs in a northerly direction towards and some quarter of a mile from the common lies Hazelhanger Farm. This has long been farmed by the Abbott family but most of the old cattle buildings have been converted into private accommodation following the change to arable farming. Most years during the spring and early summer, the area in front of the farm cottages became a small lake formed by the flooding of the Winterbourne stream.

On retiring from the Downland doctors' practice, Dr. Jack Nickson moved into the bungalow known as Warren Down, this being built on the site of the old gravel workings. The extraction of gravel from these workings ended just prior to the start of the second world war but the old works and machinery together with trucks and rails made it an excellent if very dangerous place to play. The gravel pits flooded each year and when full provided an opportunity for swimming. The whole area of the pits has become somewhat derelict and forms a wonderful haven for all types of wild life.

CHAPTER FIFTY

RETURNING TO THE village, East Lane runs from the High Street to the original A34 road.. On the land at the rear of Braziers Farmhouse stood a collection of barns and cart sheds. As the Weaver family also farmed Rectory Farm and Church Farm, Braziers had fallen into disrepair and the paddocks at the rear, now the site of Hazeldene, grew few crops other than exceptional stinging nettles. A brick built cottage stood to the east of the farm buildings and was home to farmer John Weaver until he moved into Braziers farmhouse on the death of his mother,both his brothers Geoff and Bob having died in their forties.

Beyond this stood a row of three cottages, home at one time to Miss Hazel and Miss Morgan, the infant teachers at the school and another occupied by Mr.and Mrs. Percy Pearce. At right angles to these cottages ran another row of thatched dwellings known as Quality Court. A footpath (FP 2a) ran past the doors of these cottages and was known as the back alley which joined the High Street opposite the Forge and another path (FP 2) joined the Square at the rear of the Wheatsheaf. No trace of any of these dwellings exists today as the Hazeldene houses now cover the whole area. Quality Court and its adjoining properties facing East Lane were demolished after a fire had completely gutted the end cottage, at that time occupied by Mr. Fred Thame.

At the site of the new surgery which houses the Downland Practice stood the Hare & Hounds public house. This was owned by Messrs. Ushers Brewery of Trowbridge. The first landlord I remember was Tom Phillips whose large family was very well known in the locality. Several Landlords followed over the years until the closure of the pub, among these being Fred Holland, Gordon Howe, and Lew and Mary Watts who eventually returned to their native Wales. During the time that 'Uncle' Tom Phillips was Landlord, an annual event took place during the first week of May. This was a rook shoot when anyone who owned a gun met in the rookery in the Vicarage Park and then on to the Churchyard to shoot the season's young rooks who were by that time just beginning to fly. Those late to hatch were the lucky ones as they were still in the nest and escaped the guns. Because of their tremendous numbers, rooks had to be culled annually and several hundred would be shot in the one evening set aside for that purpose. The following evening many people gathered at the Hare & Hounds to share in the delicious rook pie which had been provided by Mrs. Phillips. This was made using just the breast portions of the young birds and made excellent eating.

The Hare & Hounds was also a favourite meeting place for the Craven Hunt. The pub and the adjoining park land opposite formed a splendid setting for such an event and was much enjoyed by the numerous foot followers. Another venue was a 'lawn' meet at the Manor, in the days of Mr. Rayner. With the coming of more major roads, hunting became more difficult and the Craven Hunt amalgamated with the neighbouring Vine Hunt, thus forming the Vine & Craven as they are known today. Meets are still held in the Chieveley area occasionally at the Blue Boar and on the Agricultural Show ground opposite Priors Court. Recently a large meeting, probably the largest ever held, took place on the Agricultural Show ground, in protest to the Government's proposed bill to ban this age old way of country life. There were over eight hundred mounted riders, several packs of hounds, together with a large crowd of supporters, estimated to be in excess of ten thousand. Hopefully their protest will enable this traditional country pursuit to continue for many years to come.

Adjoining the pub was small triangular paddock which each year was visited by a small Fair before it joined Newbury Michaelmas Fair the following week. Also at the back of this paddock was a derelict farm known as Long's which consisted of several dilapidated buildings with an entrance from what is now FP no 4.

CHAPTER FIFTY ONE

BEFORE THE END of the war the only new buildings in East Lane between the Hare & Hounds and the Oxford road were three detached dwellings and a telephone exchange. These were built for Sid Leach, Mrs. S.Shepherd (of the shop) and Mr. Faulkner. Since the war however the Lane has been developed on both sides. One house was built for Dr. J. Richards and had a small purpose built surgery attached to it and housed Chieveley's first permanent medical centre. This house was called Briars, named not after the plant but for the architect, J.Briars. This has now been renamed Mulberry House. Before Dr. Richards came to the village, we were served by Dr. Risien from East Ilsley and Dr. Abraham from Brightwalton, both of whom held surgeries in a room rented in a private house. Dr. Richards' practice flourished and soon Dr. J. Nixon and Dr. D. Arnold joined the practice and a new surgery in the High Street was built by Dick Cann.

In the early days very few pills were prescribed by doctors, most medicines being liquid based and supplied in clear bottles. The doctors visited the village twice a week and as no appointments were available, patients were seen on a first come, first served basis. This often entailed a long wait, especially if the doctor happened to be called away on an emergency.

Whilst the two doctors had a friendly relationship the various groups of patients felt that their own particular man was the best.

It was a difficult journey to either of the doctor's home surgeries in Brightwalton or East Ilsley to collect a prescription. The option was to have the medicine brought by the doctor the on his next visit to the village.. Fred Jacobs the carrier would also collect medical supplies from Newbury on a Thursday or Saturday.

Before the introduction of the National Health Service, patients requiring hospital treatment would usually be sent to Newbury District Hospital in the Andover Road where they would often be seen by their own doctor.

Long gone and almost forgotten are most of the old remedies that were employed to combat various illnesses. I recall the system of soaking the feet in very hot water to which had been added a generous amount of mustard, this being regarded as a certain cure for the common cold. Another equally uncomfortable remedy was the use of Thermogene medicated wadding. This was a type of cotton wool impregnated with a none too pleasant smelling concoction, the wadding being applied in large pads directly to the skin of the chest and back. Any form of physical exertion inducing perspiration caused the padding to irritate the skin. I can remember depositing several applications into the waste bin at school.

The name of many other cures come to mind, such as Sloane's Liniment, Carter's Little Liver Pills, Zambuk ointment, Benger's Food, Brand's Essence, Sureshield Laxatives (which Gran took on a daily basis), Elliman's Embrocation (for humans and horses), Sennapods and Ex-lax for the relief of constipation and Arrowroot powder should the reverse be required. Camphor oil was used as another chest rub and Paragoric as a relief for coughs. Bran, bread and linseed were all used to poultice boils and relieve inflamation. Chilblains were always a problem, the main remedy for these being wintergreen ointment.

Before central heating came into general use, it was not uncommon to see ladies with very unsightly blotches covering their shins, caused by sitting too close to an open fire. Another invention relatively new in the 1930's was the safety razor. My father used a cut-throat razor to shave, well into the 1940's and when the time came for me to attempt shaving, this type of razor was used with disastrous results. Electric razors then became fashionable but were of little use without an electricity supply.

Mainly due to Dennis Compton, the Middlesex and England cricketer, who advertised Brylcreem hairdressing, this was one of the most popular preparations for men's hairdressing and is still available today. Before this, the only products were vaseline or the cheaper more commonly named 'Tapoline' (water).

CHAPTER FIFTY TWO

Two semi-detached houses were erected next to the Briars, one for Ern Phillips (Tom's son) and called Crownpiece after the name of the adjoining field. The other was built for Stan Pocock, a member of another well known Chieveley family and now called 'Wilderley'. These two gentlemen formed the business of Pocock and Phillips as coal merchants and operated from the railway goods yard at Hermitage where they employed several staff including Stan's son Pat. In those days before the advent of oil-fired heating and in the absence of mains gas they built up a very good business delivering coal and coke over a wide area. Almost every town and village with a railway station provided a yard for a coal merchant. Coal would be purchased by the truck load directly from the pit and delivered by goods train to the merchant. On arriving at its destination, the guards van would be uncoupled from the rear of the train and the trucks of coal for delivery shunted into a siding, the guards van having been recoupled the train would continue on its journey. At most village stations the trucks of coal or coke would then have to be hauled manually and emptied by hand into the various storage bays. Each truck contained several tons of fuel but when started into motion, usually by the use of a crowbar as a lever between the face of the rail and wheel, the load could be pushed by several men, each truck having its own lever operated braking device. The fuel would then be weighed off by hand into one hundredweight sacks for delivery to the householder. Merchants would often offer a better price to the customer in the autumn to encourage them to stock up before the winter.

Local railway stations also carried a large amount of freight, smaller items being stowed in the guards vans of passenger trains. Farmers sent milk to town in churns, the empties being returned the following day. It was not unusual to see wooden crates full of chickens and other agricultural goods piled up on the station platform. Passengers bicycles and prams were also conveyed in the guards van usually for the sum of one penny or two pence.

During the hunting season horses would sometimes be entrained at their local station to journey to the station nearest the meet. This journey being carried out in reverse at the end of the day, sometimes in darkness.

CHAPTER FIFTY THREE

NORTH ON THE old Oxford road stands a brick built house the home of the first petrol pump in the area. In the mid-thirties however, Mr.Fulcher at Hill Cafe, Shepherds in the High street and Mrs. Wells at Worlds End had petrol pumps installed to supply the needs of the ever increasing number of motor vehicles.

Next comes Fir Tree farm, the home of the Illsley family, who have in recent years incorporated the neighbouring Ashfields farm and Downs farm. They are one of the last local farmers to run a dairy herd.

During the war a large bomb fell in the field opposite the farm. This resulted in broken windows and some damage to the brickwork, with shrapnel being spread over a large area, some of which was picked up on the tennis court of Coombe House and also in the garden at our cottage. Also in the field opposite the farm (the Crownpiece) was the only time I ever witnessed ploughing being carried out by steam engine. Two engines were stationed one on each side of the field to be cultivated, a plough (three furrows I think) was then drawn by a winch operated by steel hawsers between the two machines, which would then travel forwards the width of the plough after each traverse until the field was completed I assume that the headlands were then cultivated either by horse or by tractor drawn plough.

Down End lane goes from the chestnut tree to join with the old A34 road. Opposite the chestnut tree stands Down End House, for many years the home of the Martin-Atkins family. This house was modernised by Miss Martin-Atkins' relative Mrs.Duffield.. Adjoining this property is Sun Hill farm, which was tenanted in the 1930's by Mr. Webber, a typical yeoman farmer seldom seen without boots and gaiters, moleskin breeches and smock and sporting large white 'muttonchop' whiskers. Large families were the order of the day, and the Webbers were no exception with two boys and three girls. Son Tom was a carpenter and operated from the barn at Sun Hill. Leon was music master at Priors Court School, organist and choir master at St. Mary's Church, a post which after his marriage to Vi he shared with her and which she has continued for many years, still now on a part time basis. Sister Annie was a dress maker and had a business in the Arcade in Newbury. Mimm the other sister worked for the S.E.B in Oxford road Newbury which is now the site of the new Waitrose Supermarket. The other sister Kate, married Reg (Taffy)Wardman and lived in a cottage known as Linley . Reg was a house repairer and great talker and used expletives almost every other word. He once felted, battened and re-tiled the roof of Braziers Farmhouse with no scaffold other than a ladder. At that time scaffolding consisted of wooden poles lashed together with wire ropes and the cross members being oak putlogs which were let into the brickwork at one end and rested on the scaffold at the other, scaffold boards then being placed on these bearers. What today's Health & Safety Executive would have to say is not known.

One of the pair of cottages next door to "Linley" is "Sunnyside" home of Derek and Pam Leach, another Chieveley family going back many generations. Derek was employed by Dick Cann before entering business on his own in the early 1960's as a painter and decorator until his recent retirement.

CHAPTER FIFTY FOUR

THE LANE RUNNING off to the left is called Morphetts Lane (FP no.16) , after the family who originally lived in the large house. Beyond this house was another farm known as Down End farm, which has been a private residence for many years. On the corner with Down End lane is another smallholding called Henrietta Farm, once owned by Mr. and Mrs. Payne, they kept chickens, ducks and geese and did quite a good trade selling eggs and a certain young school boy used to be petrified,having been sent to buy eggs, of being chased by a flock of honking geese.

Beyond the house a paddock stretches down to the A34. During the war years a wooden building stood in this paddock and during the summer months housed many Londoners who came on working holidays doing general farm work for the war effort. This became a very noisy and lively place during their time of residence.

On the main road going north was yet another smallholding now known as Broomdown Cottage.home to Arthur and Dennis Illsley and their sister all being of modest stature.. Dennis took part in the Airborne landings at Arnhem and unfortunately suffered the loss of both his legs.. On his return to civilian life he worked as a clerk for Dick Cann. He had a wonderful sense of humour and was often asked the question why, when having artificial legs fitted, he had not had them made longer to give him some added height. His reply was that he had no wish to hit his head on the doorpost. This farm is now incorporated into Fir Tree farm.

The A34 road which was one of the major north to south routes in the country has now been re-routed some distance to the east and at the present time major works are taking place to divert it under the M4 motorway linking it to the new Newbury bypass.

Beyond Broomdown cottage stood Broomdown House owned by Col. and Mrs. West. This in later years became a hotel called 'The Open Country' before it burned down. The site is now a residential housing estate. Beyond this is a mobile home and caravan company. Next is the former home of Mr. and Mrs. Sam Stirland who ran the Filling Station and built the adjoining garage. This site now houses a bus company and a haulage company. The next property, formerly a garage owned and run by George Simpson and his father is now a double glazing factory. At the rear of this factory is the entrance to 'Orchard Park' one of the first residential mobile home sites in the area since upgraded to include many large 'Park' homes.

Beyond the road to Peasemore is 'Cross Lanes' farm which was owned by Mr. Bell and latterly by his daughter. The Parish boundary being marked by the wall between this farm and the Langley Hall public house.

CHAPTER FIFTY FIVE

A major change to the life of the inhabitants of Chieveley in the middle of the 1930's was the coming of electricity to the village, making life much easier for everyone but depriving the shops such as Shepherds and Prismalls of the sale of paraffin oil and candles, the former being delivered to customers to supply their lighting and often cooking needs. Incidentally the cans of paraffin sometimes as many as ten or more would be carried in the same delivery van as the bread and groceries. Although usually placed in front of or on the passenger seat, the smell of paraffin was often quite prevalent inside the vehicle. On the return journey the van would be contain empty cans, these to be refilled at the shop and taken back on the next delivery.

Bread was delivered to the door in open baskets for the customer to make his or her choice, it not being unknown for the lady of the house to handle several of the (unwrapped) loaves before making her final choice. Especially delicious were Shepherd's dough cakes and lardy cakes. Lardy cakes are still being made and sold in the shop, but no one seems to know the reason for the demise of the delicious dough cake or the whereabouts of the original recipe. A serious loss to mankind if ever there was one. The shop and post office is no longer run by the Shepherd family but they still operate the bakery on a wholesale basis, supplying bread and cakes to outlets over a very wide area.

The main sewerage system was installed in the 1970's and whilst septic tanks and soakaways in our chalk subsoil worked quite well, the advent of washing machines and the installation of bathrooms and w.c's, increased the use of water and most dwellings were connected to the new system. The treatment works are sited in the North Heath road near the Ford. This works also treats sewerage from the adjoining village of Hermitage and Hermitage Camp. Some ten years after its installation the works were almost doubled in size to enable it to treat the additional volume from the various housing estates which have sprung up and presumably will be able to cope with the effluent from the proposed development of two sites in Hermitage, of some two hundred and fifty houses,

The village, as with the rest of Britain, experienced many changes during the war years. However the only war time fatalities due to enemy action were three cows as a result of bombs dropped in the Chieveley Fields area near Bussock Wood. Two were killed outright and another a Guernsey by the name of 'Stroudie' survived being hit by shrapnel for several weeks but eventually had to be humanely destroyed..

Another war time incident took place on the same day that Newbury was bombed when St.John's Church, Raymonds' Almhouses and Eastfields School were destroyed with considerable loss of life. The same plane flew over Chieveley when the harvest was under way in a field adjoining Gidley lane. Some of Weaver's men together with Geoffrey Pocock and my father (local gardeners were assisting with the harvest) were building a rick and came under machine gun fire from the German plane. Needless to say the rick was quickly evacuated. At the same time I was some three hundred yards distant, leading a horse ('Tinker') with a cart load of sheaves towards the rick and took cover under the cart laying over the axle as the old horse plodded onwards towards the rick. The enemy plane flew over so low that the faces of the crew were clearly visible from the ground and when the shooting began I clearly remember thinking that my twelve years on earth were about to come to an abrupt end. Later that year another stick of some ten smaller bombs landed in Bussock Wood near to Kites Abbey.. These did little damage, in fact Douglas Faithful and myself were the first to find the craters several days after the bombs were dropped, nobody seemingly having heard them explode.

In the early part of the war an RAF Spitfire nose-dived into the field just beyond Elm Grove farm cottages causing a huge crater and killing the unfortunate pilot, who it is believed was a New Zealander. This crash really brought home to the local residents the dangers of aerial warfare. John Cann from the Post Office was at that time flying Spitfires and he also lost his life in a tragic crash later in the war. Some months after the Spitfire crash a Wellington bomber made a forced landing in the field near Beedon Common plantation, finishing up with its nose buried in the trees. Fortunately the crew all escaped unhurt.

Also at this time many of the young men from the village were serving in the various branches of the armed forces. Being only nine years old at the outbreak of the second world war I did not know many of these personally and only made their acquaintance on their return to civvy street, when once again they took up local employment and joined in the many sporting activities. The war memorial at St.Mary's church bears the names of eight men from the village who lost their lives,the only one known to me being John Cann.

CHAPTER FIFTY SIX

IN THE YEARS before the second world war, the village was a very
closely knit community where the majority of the inhabitants were
born, married, lived and worked together in or near the village. A
marked difference from the residents of the village today who often
travel many miles to their place of employment. After the war,
farming was still the main source of employment but the coming
of mechanisation meant that far fewer men were required to work
the land. This coincided with the growth of many new industries
resulting in larger wage packets and better standards of living and
allowed many more people to afford the luxury of a car, something
which before the war would have been a very rare thing indeed, a
bus or bicycle being the only form of transport. The motor car was
instrumental in giving most people freedom of movement and travel
opportunities, and soon became a way of life.

The tied cottage system whereby the employer would provide a
cottage, usually fairly primitive, rent free to the employee, would allow
landowners to dictate conditions of employment to their workforce.
With the gradual shift to industrial employment this system has
virtually disappeared. I remember the time when my father who was
employed at Coombe House as a gardener, approached his employer

Mr. Dallin with some trepidation to ask for a ten shillings a week rise (50 new pence) to add to his weekly wage of £3. "Yes" said Mr. Dallin, "that will be all right Martin, but as you live in the cottage rent free I shall have to charge you ten shillings a week rent". Until that time I had not fully understood the meaning of the expression 'status quo'.

The motor car also allowed folk to go on holiday and visit all sorts of places rather than just the resorts only accessible by bus or train. Little did we realise at that time that in a few years most of us would be forsaking our seaside holidays in Britain in favour of more exotic climes in every corner of the world thanks to the introduction of air travel.

With the inception of television, and the arrival of the first television sets, normally a large cabinet with a screen measuring 9" offering black and white pictures on one channel, family life became very different..What I wonder would be the reaction of my grandparents' generation who had only oil lamps, solid fuel cooking and no indoor sanitation to the high-tec lifestyle of today. Many of my age group no doubt have yet to understand the complexities of the text message and so forth. I also wonder what our reaction would be if only we could look forward another seventy years to see what will have happened by then.

Another major change which took place in the village after the war was the boom in the building industry. As the prospects of increased income became available the opportunity to own one's house became a reality and in consequence most villages increased in size at an alarming rate. Not only did new families move into the village but as similar housing became available elsewhere many members of families who had been the mainstay of the village for hundreds of years, moved away. This fact being partly due to the planning authorities not making available starter homes to allow younger family members to settle in their own environment. Chieveley, in common with many villages in the area, was a particularly desirable place for development.

The effect of this has brought new blood and new ideas into the village. However well intended some of these new ideas may be, they have to be integrated with a degree of local historical knowledge and on the whole I believe that the system works well.

CHAPTER FIFTY SEVEN

TIME HAS ALSO brought many changes to the habits of village residents, one of the largest of these being in its taste in food and drink. Taking drink first, a farm labourer or working man would adjourn to one of the three local public houses namely, 'The Hare & Hounds', 'The Wheatsheaf' or the ;''Red Lion' where on offer would be 'mild' or 'bitter' both drawn from wooden barrels and usually kept in the cellar and 'light' or 'brown' ale supplied in bottles. If a lady should enter a public house, and very few did, their drink would often have been 'port and lemon' or perhaps for the more adventurous 'gin and orange' or gin and lime, not to be compared with the extensive range of drinks now sold today. Beer in those days would cost only a few pence per pint as against some £2. 50 or more, for the equivalent drink today..

In the early days many public houses sold only beer and wine and only obtained a licence to sell spirits when the demand increased. Very few could offer more than a bag of crisps or a sandwich in the way of food. A far cry from today when almost every public house offers an extensive menu in a comfortable restaurant. Licensing hours were strictly adhered to and many a public house customer has beaten a hasty retreat by way of a rear entrance when the local "bobby" entered the front door at closing time. The landlord's cry of "time ladies and gentlemen please!" has now been replaced by the sign 'open all hours'. Also some of the well known public houses have gone and we are left with just one - the Red Lion,the name of which has been further enhanced by the addition of "Ye Olde" as a prefix. This I believe took place when the owner was Mr. Granville Martin (no relation) When offering directions to a traveller who was new to the area, pubs were used as a landmark, often 'carry on this road until you come to the ....pub, then left at the ..... and so on'. Sadly the demise of so many public houses makes this form of direction used less often.

Tastes in food have also changed dramatically with the large supermarkets offering a vast range to suit everyone. These have virtually replaced the village grocer. Pre-packed goods with sell by dates and labels listing all the ingredients (most with unpronounceable names) have become the norm for today's shopper, many placing their orders on the internet. This makes shopping much easier than the days when one stood at the shop counter whilst the assistant rushed hither and thither to complete an order. However today's over zealous attitude to hygiene has meant that one seldom has the pleasure of watching a large cheddar cheese being cut to required size using a cheese wire or bacon being sliced to order to the required thickness, knowing that a large percentage of the weight would not be added water. Dry goods such as rice, flour and the like were all sold loose and weighed out as needed. Sweet jars lined the shelves and sweets were sold by the ounce. Although some tobacco was packeted, "black shag" and some pipe tobaccos were sold loose and chewing tobacco came in a rope- like coil and was cut to order. Biscuits were sold direct from tins measuring about 12 inches square each containing about seven pounds of biscuits. These would be weighed out according to the customer's requirements, each variety being priced separately. Once the tin was nearly empty this meant that a collection of broken pieces remained which would be sold at greatly reduced cost. It was common therefore to hear the customer ask for "half a pound of broken biscuits please".

The Palmer family of Priors Court were the owners of the world famous Huntley & Palmer Biscuit company of Reading. At the time when the average factory worker's wage was fifteen shillings per week (75pence) Huntley & Palmer's employees received two pounds and fifteen shillings per week. The two pounds being broken biscuits and the rest in cash.

CHAPTER FIFTY EIGHT

GROCERS SOLD LITTLE in the way of fresh vegetables for most people grew as much as they could themselves, but most shops offered various types of fruit,. this of course when it was in season unlike today when supplies are obtained world wide all year round. Despite the choices now available few who remember the succulent taste of home cured bacon cut from a joint hanging in the larder often more fat than lean, will ever forget it. Mutton was often on the menu, delicious hot or cold with home made pickle. What I wonder happens to the older sheep these days, as one only ever sees lamb on offer. Home produced pork dripping was another delight to recall and from the butcher quantities of beef suet to form one of the main ingredients for dumplings and suet crust pastry for steak and kidney puddings and apple puddings. Sadly all these are long gone together with our own village butcher's shop.

The butter sold was often produced locally, being weighed out and then formed into a neat block by the use of butter pats - two small wooden boards with handles approximately 5" x 3". Occasionally the butter pat was impressed with a picture of a cow or something similar which would then leave an imprint on the butter. The taste is one that is not easily forgotten and by far surpasses today's supplies which mostly come from the far side of the world.

Milk although not often supplied by the grocer was also of the natural or full cream variety. Cream was supplied at the local dairy and as there was little call for the resulting 'skim milk' this was fed to the pigs. Again a far cry from today when people shun the thought of high cholesterol milk and the fitness fanatics drink only what was previously considered to be a waste product. During the war years it was illegal for the dairy farmer to produce cream, however as most of my leisure time was spent at Church Farm the occasional taste of this delicacy did sometimes find its way on to the table of Coombe House Cottage. This was usually in quarter or half pint tubs which like all cream produced, involved a great deal of manual work. A Lister separator was used, a cylindrical container holding four to five gallons of milk which in turn fed down to a hand operated machine from which flowed skimmed milk for pigs and from another spout, a steady but small flow of thick cream. A back breaking task but the fruits of the labour when eaten with home grown srawberries made it all worth while.

Eggs were mostly what are now termed 'free range' with the exception of the battery hens at Pointers Close and chickens had the free run of most farm yards. They were fed on 'tail wheat' this being the left over wheat from the threshing machine the best of the wheat having gone for flour production. The chickens would forage far and wide only returning to the hen house in the evening where they would be shut in to protect them from being taken by the fox. Very few chickens in those days would have tasted the layers pellets fed to today's birds and although the eggs tasted good, hens would often make nests in various parts of the farm yard which could result in a new nest not being discovered for some time,and being shared by several hens it could contain a large number of eggs, hence the fact that the name 'fresh eggs' was not always correct.

Bread straight from the local baker's oven was another treat to enjoy. This was often made from locally grown and milled wheat flour, with fat, sugar,yeast and salt being the only other items used. Bread today contains a whole list of additives to the wheat which has originated in Russia, Canada and the USA as it appears that after centuries of use, wheat grown in our country is not of the right type and is fit only for cattle feed. Another delight were the jam doughnuts made in the bakehouse at Shepherds. The doughnut specialist was Fred Butler and I well remember waiting for these golden brown wonders to be removed from the pan of steaming fat, rolled in caster sugar and filled with raspberry jam, impatience often resulting in a burnt mouth. Those were the days.

Other foods available, again in season, were field mushrooms which seemed to abound in many of the local fields, regrettably no more because of the absence of livestock and the change to mainly arable farming. What breakfast could possibly compare to a plate of fried mushrooms which has entailed rising from bed at the crack of dawn to harvest them, not that they had to be picked at such an early hour, but if you were not there at that time ,someone else would be, and this excellent treat would finish up on the wrong breakfast table. Certainly a case of 'the early bird catching the mushroom'. Today the change in farming practices and demise of most of the dairy herds means that many of the fields in which the mushrooms grew have been ploughed and put to use for cereal production. Occasionally mushrooms would appear in vast quantities in unusual places. One such crop appeared in a field of oat stubble close to New Sheds, whilst another year in a meadow at Elm Grove Farm they grew in such profusion that it was possible to fill a large basket without moving more than a few yards. This type of mushroom crop seemed to be a 'one off' and was not repeated. Before the advent of the mechanical hedgetrimmer many of the hedgerows tended to be overgrown and besides being a wonderful haven for all forms of wild life, provided many a household with blackberries, rosehips and crab apples for their jams and jellies. Also, in the autumn another bounty was on offer in the form of walnuts, chestnuts and hazelnuts, even if some of these trees did happen to be on private property.

Various forms of wild life also found its way on to the dinner table. Rabbits, apart from those caught at harvest time, were often available and many an unfortunate bunny met its end by placing its head in the wire noose of a snare or falling victim to the owner of an accurate catapult. The odd pheasant or hare occasionally became part of the family diet but on the whole there was no poaching carried out on a large scale neither were there many keepers employed in the area.

Large scale shooting syndicates were not yet in place. Chieveley must always have been a fairly law abiding place for our last resident local policeman left the village before the start of the second world war.

Hares in those days were very plentiful and on any walk around the village they could be seen "boxing" or chasing aimlessly about. The sight of a hare today is very rare indeed. Many species of bird have almost disappeared, particularly the plover or peewit. These ground nesting birds gathered together in flocks of many thousands. Alas only the occasional pair is seen today. Another bird to fall victim to modern farming methods is the skylark, a bird which seemed to spend its day spiralling up into the sky and singing continuously. The starling massed in large flocks of many thousands and all seemed to twist and turn as one, a truly amazing sight.

The cheeky sparrow, both house sparrow and hedge sparrow or dunnock, were so numerous as to be a menace, living in hordes in farmyards and cottage gardens. Unfortunately their numbers are also declining. Blackbirds still seem to flourish as does the song thrush. The one bird that has increased at an alarming rate is the ring or collar dove, not a particularly attractive bird with a somewhat raucous call, its only redeeming feature being that it does very little damage to crops. The wild pigeon goes from strength to strength and in the absence of fields of kale and root crops grown to feed cattle, turns its attention to crops of cabbage, brussel sprouts etc., in domestic gardens and to oil-seed rape crops on the farms. Years ago these birds were shot in vast numbers by farmers. The farmers would often pay a man who would erect a hide in a crop field and he would set up 'decoys' to attract the flocks of wild pigeons and would shoot many hundreds in a single day. It must have been a very lonely and sometimes cold and wet experience to spend the day crouched in a hide consisting of a few sheets of sacking and branches.

Badgers used to occupy setts in the Grove Road and at the 'Beeches' in Gidley Lane. These setts are no longer active but a certain number of these animals must still be in the area, as one often sees them at the road side having been hit by a passing vehicle.

Hedgehogs do a grand job of work in the gardens, where they keep slugs and snails at bay, and thankfully there are still a good number of these small beasts. Prior to mechanisation a local farmer would often hire gangs of travelling gypsies to hoe the crops during the spring and summer months. It was said that a delicacy of the gypsies was roast hedgehog. By all accounts the hedgehog was wrapped in wet clay and baked in the camp fire. The spines then came away when the clay was removed. The meat was reputed to have tasted like pork, but the writer has no first hand knowledge of this.

Although not an animal for the pot, moles were prolific and when caught in any numbers would be skinned and the pelts nailed to a board to dry. Rabbit skins were also saved and hung up to dry. These skins together with old rags, bones etc would be sold to the "Rag and Bone man" who would visit the village several times a year. These would be taken away and the skins eventually used in the fashion industry, the bones for glue and fertiliser and the rags possibly recycled as felting materials.

CHAPTER FIFTY NINE

MANY CHARACTERS HAVE lived in the village during my lifetime. A few who come to mind are Tom Belcher, who answered to the nicknames of 'THB' 'Green' or 'Nonnie'. I have seen Tom playing bar billiards in the Red Lion with a live bantam cockerel perched on his head.

On another occasion when he owned a greyhound this dog was involved in racing the length of the village hall and back again as a challenge against Derek Leach. This challenge not only took place inside the hall but during the time a dance was underway. This caused great excitement for all those present. The match resulted in a win for Derek 'Humphrey' Leach , who although handicapped by the consumption of more Usher's bitter than was good for him, managed to win by several yards. This was mainly due to his using the front of the stage to assist his turn at the far end of the course. Another contributing factor being that the poor dog whose claws were quite long was unable to obtain any grip on the glass-like surface of the dance floor.

Not all the dances in the Memorial Hall were such enjoyable occasions. Often opposing sections of the American Military would use this venue to settle their differences, although fortunately they were usually concluded outside the building. A contingent of American Military police were stationed at Donnington and a great deal of their time was spent in and around the public houses of Chieveley. Another incident which I recall was a fight between two women probably over the attentions of a John Wayne or Gary Cooper lookalike. Halfway through a particular dance these two, obviously not local girls, set about trying to remove each other's hair and clothing. The band immediately started to play the National Anthem to which all in the room stood still, however the two assailants were apparently not patriotically minded and continued the affray, thus giving everyone standing still a much better view of the proceedings. Unlike the dog race I do not know the result of this match.

Tom Belcher was an enthusiastic drinker and spent many hours in the Wheatsheaf where his favourite tipple was 'mild and bitter'. One evening at a dance in the Recreation Centre when John Phillips and myself were running the bar, we gave Tom a tonic water to test, informing him that he was drinking gin and tonic. After consuming several of these he had great difficulty in walking from the bar, being fully convinced that he had consumed half a bottle of gin.

Bill 'Smiler' Belcher was a brother of Tom and worked many years for Weavers the farmers. On his retirement he took on the job of delivering newspapers locally. He was always dressed in turned down wellington boots and an old brown overcoat in the pocket of which he always carried a potato, which he claimed kept him free from illness. This may have worked as he once appeared on television as 'the oldest local paperboy in the area' being then over 80 years of age. His outfit was completed with a rather tatty cap with a broken peak.

One day after completing his deliveries, Bill, probably feeling unwell, sat down in the Bus Shelter at Church Corner, where sadly he passed away, and was found by some villagers. Joe Belcher, another brother, came past on the Maypole side of the road some minutes later, and someone came across to inform him that Bill had died, to which he replied "Ah, I didn't think he looked too good yesterday", at which point he then carried on walking home to Downend.

I dread to think what Bill would have done if he were still delivering papers today, the sheer size and weight of the weekend editions being enough to deter even the stoutest of delivery people, who mostly use a vehicle, let alone carrying them in a canvas bag.

Billy Groves worked, I believe as stud groom, for Mr. Rayner at the Manor. We would often pass him on our way to school while he was making his way back to work after breakfast at his home in Makina Villas. As with most professional horsemen, he was somewhat short of stature with rather bandy legs covered with old style riding breeches. His outstanding feature was a very large walrus-type moustache which was silver grey in colour but with a very distinctive gingery-brown patch immediately under his nose. This we discovered later was due to his being addicted to snuff,.this being easily obtained from the local tobacconist and had the effect of discolouring his otherwise splendid facial adornment..

Another character was Jack Napper a relative of the Pearce family of Bardown. He was evacuated from London at the start of the war with his family and lived in the small cottage adjoining the butcher's shop in the Square. Jack was a sergeant in the Home Guard, he was a very short man and when armed with a Lee-Enfield rifle with an 18" bayonet attached, the weapon was almost as tall as the bearer. Jack drove a lorry for R J Free of Newbury which he brought home with him each night and the next morning as many as five or six of us who regularly biked to work, would be waiting in the Square ready to fling our 'steeds' into the rear of the lorry then scramble in the back ourselves, to save pedalling into Newbury. Even on very cold or wet days the journey in the back of an open lorry being preferable to cycling five miles.

During my time as an army cadet Eric Napper, Jack's son, was a Lance Corporal and he and I were to cycle to Newbury one Sunday afternoon to attend a Parade. Calling for Eric I was invited to sit down for a few minutes and duly sat at one end of a couch in the kitchen, only to be greeted by an almighty shout from Jack who was asleep at the time covered by an army greatcoat, and in the somewhat gloomy conditions I had managed to sit on his head.

Bill Leach (my uncle) was also rather short of stature and when holding a rifle and bayonet he and Jack Napper made a handsome pair, Jack with his Hitler-like moustache and Bill with his built-up boot necessitated by an accident in childhood. He lived with his wife

Kit at The Chalet and ran a boot and shoe repair business in a first floor shop over the garage in Pig Lane.

Bill Pearce and his wife Elsie lived at Northfields where they raised a very large family. Bill worked in the building trade for Dick Cann, as did his son 'young Bill'. He in turn started a building firm on his own account and now has become 'old Bill' while his son 'young Bill' and brother Jim continue to run the firm.

Another well known couple were Bert and Annie Winter who lived in the cottage close to the Red Lion, which is now called "Littlecote", where they raised a large family of boys. They were for many years Vergers at the Church and after Bert's death, the job was taken over by his son Arthur who, on marrying, lived in the Old Infant School cottage. Arthur carried out the position of Verger until his retirement in the middle 1980's. Most of the boys were named in a very patriotic fashion. They were Nelson, Lawrence, Stanley, Arthur then came Lesley John (Jack) and youngest son Norman. All of them played football for Chieveley but never all at the same time,. Jack being probably the best all-round sportsman the village has ever produced. Annie Winter also washed the football team's shirts and on a Monday morning a row of these garments wold appear on her washing line. How she ever managed to dry them during the wet weather I know not. The shirts were made of knitted cotton and very heavy. The necks had eyelets through which was threaded a lace, similar to that used to tie a boot or shoe, but of course no numbers or names were on these garments. The colours were green and white vertical stripes. These were the racing colours of Mr. Oscar Rayner of the Manor and he may have presented the Club with the shirts but no record of this remains. In later years the colours changed to green and white quarters.

In regard to naming children, my own grandparents, Fred and Annie Leach, both of whom were devout Methodists, christened their second son John Wesley. Their other children being William, Kathleen (my mother) and Horace.

CHAPTER SIXTY

JOHN 'FARMER JOHN' Weaver lived at Braziers Farm and ran the arable side of the farm together with the pigs at Rectory farm. A very affable character and somewhat portly, he had a passion for Chinese food, when he together with Wally Shepherd, Michael Pocock and myself would often journey to Newbury to the Laurel Restaurant, this being the first one of its kind in the area, opening during the early sixties.

Many years prior to this, leaving Coombe House cottage at around 7.30 in the morning, as I was on my way to work, I heard a cry for help coming from the pig shed to the rear of the farmyard at Rectory Farm. John had fallen near the entrance, landing in pig slurry several inches in depth and had broken his ankle. Having collected my van from the garage in Manor Lane I managed to get his considerable weight into the back of my small Ford van and duly delivered him to Newbury Hospital where no doubt the staff had to hose him down before looking at his injuries. Several years earlier, Farmer John who was a keen shot held several shoots over his land during the winter months, at which we lads were employed as beaters. One day whilst drawing a piece of kale near Church Farm quite a large number of birds took off in the direction of Green Lane where the guns were waiting. This particular day, Farmer John was sporting a brand new 12 bore shot gun purchased at some considerable expense from Turners, the Gunsmiths of Northbrook Street Newbury. He was at the end of the line when a brace of pheasants took off in the direction of Bussock Wood and although they were well out of range he let them have both barrels from his new 'piece'. For many months he was the butt of the shooting fraternity's jokes who ribbed him that he must have strained his new gun by firing at a target so far out of reach.

Bert 'Chippy' Taylor worked as head carter for Weavers and lived in one of the thatched cottages adjoining Rectory Farm. He was very partial to Morlands beer and as with most agricultural workers at that time, before the advent of television, spent many evenings at the 'local' drinking, smoking and often playing cards, dominoes and darts. Later bar-billiards became quite popular as a bar-room game. Bert was seldom seen without his short-stemmed clay pipe and always had an amusing tale to tell.

A certain horse, a grey shire by the name of Punch, was at Church Farm drawing a flat-bed cart. There being no one available to drive him back to his stable at Rectory Farm, he was given a smart slap across the rump and sent on his way homeward together with the cart. This took place early one summer evening and the poor horse, having safely negotiated the trip through the village, entered the farmyard at Rectory Farm fully expecting someone to unhitch him from the cart, unharness and feed him. Having stood patiently in the yard for some time, he then attempted to enter the stable with the cart attached, where he and the cart became hopelessly wedged and in which state they were eventually found by 'Chippy' on his way home from the pub at closing time. He with the help of my father managed to extricate Punch and all was well. However a few choice words took place between 'Church Farm and Rectory Farm' over the next few days.

I have often ridden on a cart driven by Chippy to and from Hermitage Railway station to collect goods for the farm. The Great Western Railway delivered goods to and from the station, by horse drawn wagons in Newbury Town but no such service was available in the outlying villages, and local farmers would have to arrange their own means of transportation.

Chippy also carried out the thatching of hay and corn ricks. This job was not as specialised as that done on domestic dwellings, for whereas the thatch on dwellings was intended to keep out the weather for as many years as possible, that on a rick would usually be required to last just a few months until the contents of the rick were either used for feed or threshed. Threshing usually took place during the spring months. Corn ricks were some twenty five to thirty feet high at their highest point and a long pole ladder would be used by the thatcher. The material used was wheat straw and pegged in place with split and twisted hazel branches.

Chippy had a dog by name of Toby who was a white terrier type with legs somewhat longer than today's Jack Russell. This dog mastered the art of climbing the ladder as it lay up the rick and would join his master at the very top. He never did manage the descent and always had to be carried down.

CHAPTER SIXTY ONE

Mr. Thomas was landlord at the Red Lion now known as Ye Olde Red Lion. He was a large imposing figure of a man, who besides running the pub, had a cycle repair business. He displayed a notice in his workshop window which read "The man who lends pumps and tools is out". He drove a large motorbike and sidecar and rumour has it that he went into Camp Hopson's outfitters to buy a 'motorcycling cap' only to be told by the assistant that they stocked only normal caps, one of which was duly proffered. Mr. Thomas tried this on with the peak at the back, exclaiming "This is exactly what I want!", and purchased the said headgear over which he always wore an enormous pair of goggles.

Another character worthy of mention is Bob Halls who lived at North Heath and was gardener at the North Heath House. During the war years he would often show his famous trick to visiting US airmen and customers at the Wheatsheaf. Although not a tall man he had the amazing ability of picking up a sixpenny piece from the floor with his mouth, and his hands behind his back. I have seen him pocket a good many sixpences,.the sixpence in those days being smaller than the one pence coin of today and Bob at that time would have been some sixty years of age. His son Bob, who lives at Downend was gardener at Downend House, continuing his father's occupation, but not as far as I am aware his amazing and athletic feat.

Jockey Hughes lived in a cottage at Horsemoor next to Slip Leach (these cottages made into one by Dr. Nickson). Jockey rode a motorcycle with a large box-type sidecar attached. This was often piled high with cut birch branches in connection with his job as fence builder at most of the local race courses. The floor boards of the bedroom in his cottage were not in a very good state of repair and one night the leg of the bed went through leaving quite a large hole. The ceiling was of the exposed beam type so it was possible to see into the bedroom from the living room below. The bed was duly moved over and for a long time, before repairs were carried out, the morning cups of tea would be handed up through the hole in the ceiling.

Bill Bennett lived with his family in the first of the council houses at Downend later to become known as Northfields, and was for many years the village road man, and kept the verges, hedges and ditches in superb order,. his only mechanical aid being a three-wheeled barrow which contained his hand-tools. His 'stretch' ran from the cross-roads to the Beedon Common plantation and all the lanes in the village .

Every so often these roads would be tarred and gritted. The tar-boiler, a huge black device with a firebox below was used to heat the tar, and a winch was used to raise the wooden barrels of tar for emptying into the top of the boiler. When heated the tar was transferred to a tank on the back of the steam roller and in turn sprayed onto the road surface. This was then covered with grit either spread manually by shovel or directly from the rear of a gritting lorry. The steamroller then rolled the surface which would create a good hard wearing road. The smell of the hot tar, the smoke and noise leave a lasting memory. The gravel to be used on the road was piled on the verges in various locations throughout the village several weeks before the work was to take place. These heaps of gravel made excellent sport for approaching at full speed on a bicycle, the bicycle being brought to a sudden halt, the rider being propelled over the handle-bars to land on top of the heap. This was enjoyed by all the village boys but Bill Bennett did not share their enthusiasm on seeing

his tidy gravel heaps being spread about and soon gave vent to his
feelings by chasing the culprits. I have never seen a leather belt with
a brass buckle removed and put to use in such a short space of time.
Another pet hate of his was the fact that the Downend pond wall
(now fenced off) was used by the local 'boy racers' on their bikes,
the boldest of whom frequently rode along its top at an alarming rate.
Another favourite trick was to ride bicycles sitting on the handlebars
facing backwards, not as easy as it sounds but in this position races
were very often the order of the day. This was of course long before
the day of the 'mountain bike' and the subsequent daring exploits of
their riders.

CHAPTER SIXTY TWO

MY EARLIEST RECOLLECTION of local carriers was Ernie Jacobs of Peasemore who travelled from his home to Newbury every Thursday and Saturday. He would fetch and carry all sorts of goods and during the winter months his homeward trip was made mostly in darkness. He drove an old grey horse and covered wagon and the old horse must have known every inch of the road which consisted of a round trip of almost twenty miles. For the carrier to call a card or board with the letter 'J' clearly written upon it would be hung on a garden gate or stuck into an adjoining hedge on a stake. Ernie retired in the late 1930's and the round was taken on by his brother Fred. He boasted a brown motor van. This had a let down tailboard at the rear supported by chains at each side. This tailboard made a wonderful place for schoolboys to ride upon when not loaded with chicken crates or other bulky items, and provided Fred did not see them creeping up behind his van before he moved off. Fred eventually retired during the war and no one took on the carrier's job.

Another weekly visitor to the village during the late 1930's and into the war period, was Johnnie Green from Newbury who, with his daughter Eunice drove a large green van, from the rear of which they sold a vast array of goods including paraffin oil which was still in great demand for heating, lighting and cooking. Johnnie was a small man who always wore a grey warehouse coat and a dark blue beret. He was a very accomplished ventriloquist and would hold amusing conversations with his "little man who lived in the van". As children we would gather by the open rear doors and wonder at his conversation with the "little man" who was never seen but always heard.

One outstanding name from schooldays was Leslie or Leso, Hide. He was a year or two older than myself as his younger brother Rodney was in my class. The family lived in Curridge and the children walked to school each day. Leso was a big strong lad for his age, but not of an aggresive nature. However he was held in great respect by many of the younger boys. During one playtime most of the boys were in the Rec playing farms. Two were 'horses' dragging a large branch and the carter was driving them with string for reins. Leso arrived late on the scene and wanted to join in the game and be the farmer, only to be told by some brave individual that he could be a chicken. This did not suit and he soon set about most of the other participants. One day, some two weeks before we broke up for the summer holidays and the time when Leso was due to leave school, he did something to offend Mr. Tanner the Headmaster and was sent down to wait outside the Private Room. When the Headmaster arrived with his cane to dish out the punishment, Leso had cleared off home by way of the girls' cloakroom, and he never came back. I cannot recall ever seeing him from that day onwards. A year before this time, he had been on the farm during threshing, always a dangerous place to be with belts and pulleys on the machine flying in all directions. Being somewhat inquisitive, he stuck his finger into a hole in the side of the threshing machine. Hastily removing it he discovered that the end had been chopped off.

CHAPTER SIXTY THREE

MANY MEMORABLE PEOPLE have been involved with the various sporting activities which took place in the Village. The Chieveley Football Club was once a force to be reckoned with and records show numerous successes against such Clubs as Newbury, Thatcham, Hungerford and Lambourn. In the early years, players including Sid and Albert Leach, Des Broad, Jack Martin and Lewis Winter were much in evidence. Late in the 1930's and 40's came Bob Weaver, Lawrence, Jack, Nelson, Arthur and Norman Winter, then in the 1950's another successful team comprised Reg Goodchild, David and Derek Leach, John Winter, Bill Martin, Alan Lawrence, Doug Faithfull, John Phillips and Bill Lynch. All these teams achieved many victories both in local Cup and League matches. Sadly the game in the village is in decline and the facilities are now let to other clubs.

Unfortunately the game of cricket has suffered the same fate and from its former days of glory at Priors Court and two other grounds in the village is no longer played at Chieveley. In the days of such stalwarts as Sid Leach, Harry Booker and Bill Martin (former

Captains) Harry 'Jock' Baines, Eric Maule, Jack Winter, Bob
Brockway, John Troughton, Brian and Richard Atkins and also in the
earlier days at Priors Court, Chieveley commanded a certain respect
and boasted facilities which were the envy of visiting teams. All this
came to an end in the late 1960's and early 70's when the interest
waned. Although several attempts have been made to resurrect the
club, the ground is now let to outside teams and the former excellent
standard of 'the square'and outfield is totally lost.

Two more players who must receive a mention are Rodney and
Gerald Palmer whose home was Priors Court. The former was an
excellent fast bowler who played for Hampshire (and Chieveley when
available) and who later lived with his wife at Peasemore Manor.
His brother Gerald was a fearless wicket keeper who, although he
wore glasses stood right up to the stumps regardless of the speed
of the delivery and also the fact that in those days the pitches could
be very uncertain in bounce and pace. In his earlier days he kept
wicket for Winchester College and was also an excellent opening bat
and was for many years the President of the Chieveley Cricket Club.
After leaving Priors Court, he moved to Bussock Mayne where he
was responsible for the major landscaping works which took place in
the grounds there. He also represented Winchester as a Member of
Parliament for many years.

Two fascinating cricketing memories come to mind worthy of
mention. The first concerns Malcolm 'Nerkie' Pearce who was
batting number eleven for Chieveley in an evening Cup Final match ,
against Compton which was played at West Ilsley, in the late 70's. He
normally went in last with a batting average of no more than ten runs
in a season. In this game Chieveley needed five runs to win with one
ball remaining to be bowled. To everyone's delight and amazement
he hoisted the ball over the square leg boundary for a six to win us
the tournament and Cup. As well as being named man of the match
I recall that he was not sober for several days.

A second unusual incident took place during the time that Chieveley
Cricket Club were playing on the recreation ground opposite the
School. Bonar Cobb who lived in the Round House was batting at
the village end. He had little or no hair and in ducking to avoid a fast
delivery was hit on top of the head. The ball which was travelling at

great speed came off the top of his head and landed beyond the long leg boundary. This is the only time I have ever witnessed six leg-byes being scored in any fashion let alone off the batsman's head. Apart from a slight bruise he suffered no injury from the blow.

With the coming of the Recreation Centre to the village a Tennis Club was formed and two hard courts laid. Up until this time only a few privately owned grass courts were in being, and from these several players successfully made the transition to hard courts. Among these were Wally Shepherd and Leon Webber, both well past middle age but still quality players. Other keen players included Jack McDonald from Radnall Farm, Bonar Cobb, David Abbott, and Philip Cockeril, together with many others. A wooden pavilion was built adjacent to the Courts. During the last few years additional Courts have been constructed and a permanent brick built pavilion has been erected on the site of the earlier building and the Club appears to be going from strength to strength.

The Recreation Centre also has a playground area with various items of equipment for the younger children. Also hugely popular is the annual 'Guy' competition followed by a spectacular bonfire and firework display. Those originally responsible for what has now become a very well attended function (always held on the 5th November irrespective of the day of the week) were Tom Bower of Downs Farm, Dr. David Arnold, Derek Leach and myself. The event must now have been going strong for some twenty to thirty years. The residents of the recently constructed Middle Farm Close estate will be afforded a grandstand view of the proceedings.

This Centre was also home to the Chieveley Evergreen Club which was started many years ago by Mrs. Glover of Sevenacres and a committee of local ladies. This club until its recent demise provided tea, entertainment, outings and a Christmas lunch for the senior members of the village. This was very much appreciated and enjoyed, but as with similar organisations in adjoining villages, lost some of its former members and was no longer a viable proposition. Not so the local branch of the Women's Institute which is still a flourishing society. Another group which was very popular for some years was the Chieveley Badminton Club, a very physically demanding sport but highly enjoyable. Regretably this Club has ceased to exist because of a shortage of members.

Several of these members have now formed the far less physically demanding sport of short-mat bowls. This relatively new game has been in existence for ten years or so. The Club was formed by Mike Perry and Harry Argent and from modest beginnings has become a thriving enterprise, offering four mats and playing matches against teams from adjoining villages.

Whist drives take place occasionally in the club room at the Centre but nowhere on the scale of those held in bygone years. Before the war Mrs. Fred Leach (my grandmother) ran many whist drives, the biggest being the annual "Fur and Feather" drive in aid of the National Children's Home. One year in particular in the Memorial Hall, no less than one hundred and nine tables were in play, making four hundred and thirty six players in all. The Centre is still the main venue for functions in the village and provides changing rooms for football and cricket teams who use the grounds.

The Horticultural Society holds three shows annually in the Recreation Centre, with a large following. This Society has flourished in the village since being formed soon after the first World War, and continues to go from strength to strength, having recently changed its name to Chieveley Gardening Club. The shows initially held in a marquee in the grounds of the Manor, had one class for villagers and another for professional gardeners, who were employed at the bigger houses. After the second World War few people employed a full time gardener and the show classes were re-scheduled for "villagers" and "open". I well remember opening the envelopes containing prize money won by my father Jack Martin, who was employed as a gardener by Mr. F.T.Dallin of Coombe House. Money for 1st prize was usually six pence or one shilling for any individual class (two and a half pence or five pence) and to a small boy of six or seven years of age, represented a small fortune.

Mr. Michael Pocock of Manor Lane has indeed followed in his father's footsteps as a gardener and has excelled as a showman for many years, winning many classes at shows all over the south of England and at National level, especially in classes for his favourite sweet peas and chrysanthemums. His experience as a judge is in great demand at local horticultural shows.

Ted Brooks and his daughter Anne Croucher are generally among the winners at the shows, as are Eddie Smith and his wife. The society holds monthly meetings in the village hall on a wide range of subjects and membership of the society holds many benefits, including discount at some local garden centres.

Another well attended function over the last few years is the annual "Carols for Everyone" concert held just before Christmas. A mixed programme of carols and Christmas songs is led by St. Mary's Church Choir, accompanied by the inimitable Mrs. Webber at the piano. Mulled wine and mince pies are served to the assembled company, the hall usually filled to overflowing with parents and children.

CHAPTER SIXTY FOUR

Tremendous changes have taken place in the world of gardening over the years. Coombe House had no greenhouse and my father had to raise all the bedding plants in two large cold frames. These were brick built and measured some eight feet by eight feet by three feet high, complete with two glazed sliding covers to each of them. The soil inside these frames was excavated to about two feet below ground level and then the whole was filled with new horse manure to within a few inches of the covers. After settlement this manure was covered with a thin layer of soil and the heat generated from the rotting manure ensured sufficient temperature for seed germination. Seeds were raised in wooden trays, which were hand made, or in old wooden fish boxes obtained from fishmongers in Newbury (Macfisheries or Brindleys). These were approximately the same size as today's plastic seed trays. The soil used for seed sowing was usually sieved garden soil mixed with peat, these being the only materials available at that time, there being no multi-purpose or seed sowing composts about .. The amount of work in preparing and emptying these frames each year was a back-breaking task, the contents of the frame having to be moved by wheel-barrow. Watering was another time consuming occupation, there being no mains water available.

Every drop had to be transported to the garden from the main house by water cart, a hand drawn container holding some forty gallons, mounted on a metal frame with two iron wheels. Water was then dipped out of this container until it was approximately half empty at which time it could be tipped on its swivel mountings and emptied into buckets or watering cans.

Farm yard manure was always available in vast quantities from the local farms, usually of excellent quality and very cheap. However it would often contain a large quantity of weed seeds such as dandelion, buttercup, thistles, poppies etc. As most houses were heated by open fires a plentiful supply of soot was to hand, which after being stored for several months was a useful deterrent for slugs and snails. The same fires provided wood ash another source of fertiliser.

Coombe house garden had several large round galvanised corrugated iron rain-water tanks, these being fed from the roofs of the potting shed, wood shed and apple store. Every gallon saved in this manner, being one gallon less to be heaved from the house by water-cart. The contents of some of these tanks were enriched by the addition of a jute sack of sheep droppings suspended on a cord and this formed the main source of fertiliser for such plants as tomatoes, cucumbers, marrows etc. All this being a far cry from today's garden centres with their seemingly unending display of sprays, powders and potions to treat every kind of garden pest or disease imaginable. Things have eventually gone full circle, in as much as the EU Commissioners have now, in their wisdom, banned almost all the chemical controls that the amateur gardener had to call upon to fight the horde of garden predators. Too bad there is no longer any soot available. No doubt the plant breeders and seed suppliers have vastly improved the quality of the varieties now available, but it is sad to see some of the wellknown and much loved older variety of vegetable passing into oblivion.

Several fallacies have been handed down to gardeners by their predecessors over the years. One of the most popular being that potatoes should always be planted on Good Friday. This probably dates from the time that most people worked on the land and Good Friday being a holiday was the only available day for them to carry out this particular task. However because the date of this holiday can vary from year to year by anything up to six weeks, it rather makes a nonsense of the 'rule'.

One of Mr. Michael Pocock's beliefs is that the seed from which show onions are to be grown should be planted on Christmas morning. There may however be more in this saying that meets the eye as he certainly obtains excellent results with this plan.

The lawns at the Manor were mown by a mower drawn by a pony, this animal being fitted with leather boots to prevent damage to the turf. One set of such boots for many years adorned the wall of the bowling alley at the Hare & Hounds public house in East Lane. Motor mowers became the norm for the larger houses, especially those with a tennis court. Few cottages had lawns the garden space being used to grow vegetables and some flowers. If a small lawn was put down, a push mower would be used to keep it tidy. All mowers at this time were of the cylinder blade type. With the army of electrically powered tools, mowers, cultivators, hedge trimmers, scarifiers and so on becoming an every-day part of gardening the effort involved has been much reduced.

Sadly, new houses today have smaller gardens and as householders have so many more options as to how to spend their leisure time, the pleasure and skill of gardening is in decline, fruit and vegetables now being readily available from shops and supermarkets seven days a week, washed and neatly packaged., allowing the purchaser to avoid the frustrations of frost, heat, snow, weeds, drought and predators both above and below ground including those that fly, creep, crawl or burrow and neighbours' cats and dogs. The work in a garden is a small price to pay in return for a dish of new potatoes or peas and tomatoes picked straight from the plant.

Perhaps one day the lure of gardening will take the place of a visit to the gym or health centre. Television garden make-over programmes may even show how to carry out the necessary gardening tasks instead of painting sheds and fences blue or covering the whole area with wood or paving slabs, rather than showing the viewer which end of the spade to hold and how to sow a few seeds.

CHAPTER SIXTY FIVE

A MAJOR CHANGE WHICH affected the lives of most village people in the 1950's 60's was the introduction of "home improvement grants". These grants were made available to home owners and the owners of property occupied by their employees, to allow sanitary fittings and hot water and drainage systems to be installed. This grant provided a great deal of work for the local trades people. Two of the first cottages to be converted were those of Mr. and Mrs. Vic Hanney and Mr and Mrs Albert Leach in the High Street, between the Forge and the Methodist Chapel. This also changed my own way of life, for after installing their bathroom, Vic and Gladys kindly offered me the use of their bath on a Friday evening. This invitation was eagerly accepted and was a luxury compared with the galvanised bath in front of the kitchen range at Coombe House cottage, the water having to be heated in a wood burning copper in a shed opposite the back door. The water was then dipped out into a bucket and carried into the house for use. Afterwards the bath was emptied using the same bucket and the water disposed of on the garden. Until the late 1960's when my mother left the old home, the only water supply was a tap in the shed and a bucket-type outside toilet still in use.

With the installation of hot water systems came washing machines which were of the twin-tub design to start with, followed by fully automatic machines. Not a sad but a fond farewell to the old copper, copper stick and 'blue bag'. The washing machine era brought about many new materials in the form of nylon and similar man-made fibres. Drip dry shirts meant no more spraying with starch solutions and the electric iron saw the end of 'flat irons' which had to be heated over an open flame usually on the kitchen range. My own recollection of shirts worn to go dancing and so on were of a pattern that had separate collars requiring front and back studs to fit them together. Many a precious minute was lost on ones hand and knees looking for a dropped stud, especially on a dark evening with the aid of light from an oil lamp or candle. The difficult decision as to what one should wear was not as hard to make in those days, as the choice was much more limited. The average working man would probably possess one suit for 'best' and work clothes. Another memory is of placing the clothes taken off at night on the bed beneath the eiderdown. This not only helped keep you warm but ensured that the clothes were not freezing cold the following morning, as in the winter months they certainly would have been if left on a chair by the window.

There were no rubber gloves to protect the hands or detergents to clean the crockery, an enamel bowl on the kitchen table, filled with hot water from a kettle to which was added a handful of washing soda was the usual method of washing up.before the installation of hot water systems. Much later the advent of the dishwasher saw the end of the above methods and proved to be a great time saver, particularly as more housewives were taking on full time employment outside the home.

Likewise the washing of clothes when done by hand used Lifebuoy bar soap or Sylvan soap flakes instead of today's vast choice of soap detergent, non biological detergent, softeners, rinse aids, and pre-wash substances. Spin and tumble driers have almost seen the end of washing hanging out to dry on a Monday 'washday' morning, or witnessing the frantic dash of the housewife getting the washing in should it start to rain. Other calamities such as the clothes prop breaking or gypsy made wooden clothes pegs working loose, allowed the lines of washing to drag the ground, making it necessary to start the process all over again.

CHAPTER SIXTY SIX

PRIOR TO THE commencement of the second world War, the Chieveley parish boasted some twenty or so farms and small holdings, these being Downend, North Heath, Ogdown, Elm Grove, Fir Tree, Rectory, Longs, Church, Cross Lanes, Downs, Ashfields, Radnalls, New, Henrietta, Sunhill, Priors Court, Manor, Braziers, Bradley Court, Broomdown, Rose, Birds, Snelsmore, Copyhold, Grange and Home Farm Arlington. Now just a handful of these farms remain, only one of which runs a dairy herd. Even before the outbreak of World War II many of the smaller farms had become run down and were eventually incorporated into that owned by a neighbour. The demise of the farm horse caused by the introduction of the tractor brought about many changes and the farm work force reduced to just a few people. Although various sorts of tractor became available from the early part of the twentieth century the first I recall in the mid-30's were made by Fordson, the earlier models having spikes or 'spuds' on their rear wheels, their use being restricted to off-road work.

Next came the orange coloured Fordson which was mounted on pneumatic tyres all round, but still only had a metal seat for the driver fixed at the rear of the vehicle, exposing him to all weathers.

This model ran on paraffin fuel but had to be started manually using a separate tank to supply petrol to the engine for this purpose, the change over to paraffin being made after the engine had warmed up. Weavers were the first local farm to own one of these splendid contraptions and I recall it's registration number being BRX 60.

This tractor was driven by Ern Meadham with verve and panache which would be the envy of any of the current Formula One drivers.

After the war another such tractor was used at the Recreation Centre to pull a set of gang-mowers to cut the grass. I have spent countless hours roaring round the ground doing this job for which in the 1950's I received the magnificent sum of one shilling and six pence per hour (seven and a half pence). This work has for many years now been carried out by contractors. Another popular farm tractor of the day was the Ferguson, a relatively small machine with a tool-bar attachment at the rear, which made it suitable for use on smaller farms and on horticultural holdings. Since those days tractors have become increasingly larger and more powerful, usually fitted with air-conditioned cabs, radios (often two-way), lights and even a satellite control device, for use in crop spraying. What a joy it must be to drive one of these monsters after the discomfort experienced on the models of yesteryear. There is indeed some truth in today's farming saying "if you can't do it with a tractor, it must be impossible."

During the war years and for some years following farming was not the profitable business it was to become in the 70's and 80's when returns were high and the price of land rocketed. In the early years most farm yards and buildings had an air of unkept neglect and despair about them. Implements would often be left in the yard and left there to rot and rust and be quickly covered with nettles and brambles. The binder became obsolete, likewise threshing tackle and elevators due to the coming of the combine harvester. This also meant that the harvested corn would be piled on the floor of a purpose built grain store, doing away with the large barns that would have been a home to the grain when it was stored in jute sacks.

A practice carried out extensively prior to the outbreak of war in 1939 was allowing land to lay fallow by leaving it uncultivated, usually every fourth year. With the coming of the war the need to produce more home grown food involved the clearance and ploughing of all available land. During the last few years however, things seem to have gone full circle and farmers are paid so much an acre under the "set aside" scheme to avoid over production. Another damaging scheme was the introduction of the milk quota, which had the effect of forcing many dairy farms out of business. The restriction placed on cattle movement and slaughter has resulted in the closure of nearly all the cattle markets which were held in most country towns on a weekly basis. Market day was always the busiest day of the week, when the farmer came to town to buy, sell or just talk about the crops and animals offered for sale.

Perhaps the cost was prohibitive but before the introduction of pre-mixed concrete, most farms in winter were a particularly muddy affair. This however, would change in summer when the slightest breeze would cause clouds of dust to cover everything. Most farms had a large number of cats, but however many there were, rats and mice always seemed to proliferate. Barns and cart sheds always seemed to be cluttered up with masses of junk, either put aside in case it came in handy one day but most likely there because it was too much trouble to dispose of it. Scrap dealers would visit the area occasionally, but the prudent farmer always thought that the next dealer to call would offer him a few shillings more, so consequently the obsolete implements remained where they were. Many hand operated implements have long since vanished, such as chaff cutters, winnowers and mangel choppers. Also gone with the work horse are the magnificent sets of harness, studded with brass although I well recall many such pieces of tack being held together with binding twine. So many hundreds of relics lay buried under the houses and gardens which now occupy these old farm sites

CHAPTER SIXTY SEVEN

Whereas years ago the Berkshire accent was very pronounced, today it is seldom heard. One particular peculiarity which comes to mind was the use of the expression "old boy" spoken as ' air ol' boy' (our old boy). This would be used when referring to any male in the family, but was usually kept for the youngest member, i.e., someone's six month old son. To be called a 'good ol' boy' was considered an honour. To hear a group of locals in the public bar either discussing the weather or the merits of the football team was a rare treat, especially when they had sampled a few pints of mild and bitter. Sadly with the passing of that generation, local dialects have almost completely disappeared and many of the colourful expressions lost for ever.

In those days people came into social contact with each other at school and work and sport more than they do today, mainly because there was little in the way of transport and no television. The majority of the local children attended the village school from the age of five years until leaving at fourteen. They would then often go on to places of work together also football and cricket teams consisted of the village people., which made for a stronger communal tie. From an early age most villagers were given nicknames, although not always of their own choice. Many of these nicknames were derivatives of their christian or surnames, some from their occupation and others referred to their stature. Some however do not fall into any of the above categories and it is left to our imagination as to some of their meanings. The writer does know a good many of the meanings but feels it may be imprudent to elaborate further on this subject. The following persons have lived in the village during the last seventy or so years and I apologise for any omissions or should that read inclusions?

Mr. 'Matter' Ireland. Reg ' Tubber' Nicholls. Ron 'Curly' Nicholls. Bert 'Chippy' Taylor. Bert 'Brickie' Pearce. The Revd. 'Nonnie' Neal. Ken 'Crooner' Bosley. Brian 'Rasher' Bosley. Ronnie 'Cuckoo' Pearce. Graham 'Crankie' Woods. Nelson 'Nellie' Winter. Lawrence 'Lardy' Winter. Arthur 'Tubby' Winter. David 'Minnow' Leach. Derek 'Humphrey' Leach. Wesley 'Messer' Leach. Bill 'Wid' Leach. Ed 'Slip' Leach. Les 'Chittles' Holmes. Alec 'Nobby' Holmes. Bill 'Smiler' Belcher. Tom 'Nonny' Belcher. John 'Farmer' Weaver. Mrs. 'Granny' Holmes and Miss 'Granny'Morgan Doug 'Shake' Faithfull. . Peter 'Diver' Chapman. Frank 'Crapper' Holliday., Wally 'Shinny' Shepherd. Albert 'Doctor' Leach. Ernest 'Baker' Leach. Teddy 'Sausage' Sawyer. Bill 'Polly' Hitchins. Reg 'Sailor' Arnold. Sidney 'Jumbo' Brind. Desmond 'Ghandi' Brind. 'Bluff' Argent. Harry 'Jock' Baine. Dick 'Henry' Winter. Jack 'Jim' Pike. John 'Wink' Willoughby. Ron 'Quacker' Quelch. David 'Domer' Quelch. Willy 'Wriggle' Sprules. Bill 'Wiggle' Pearce. Reg 'Jockey' Hughes. Reg 'Taffy 'Wardman. Malcolm 'Nurkie' Pearce, 'Tosher' Merrit, 'Goozer' Kemp, Reg 'Chunky' Williams and Brian 'Plum' Booker..

In the normal course of the day, these nicknames would be used instead of the given christian name although not always in the individual's hearing.

I have to go back now and recall another character from the past who comes to mind; Bert Garrard who was gardener for Mrs. Muller who lived at Horsemoor, now Chieveley Cottage. He was a very good gardener but also had several other jobs which kept him occupied during his spare time. He always wore a gardener's green apron and a flat cap and sported a Hitler-style moustache. As well as his gardening achievements he was the village chimney sweep and could often be seen with his bundle of rods and brushes tied to his bicycle, with a large bag of soot draped over the carrier at the rear. Almost all the houses had one or more solid fuel fires and his serviceswere in great demand.

Another job he had was to cut men and boys' hair, a job which usually took place at his cottage in Horsemoor on a Saturday morning. Styles in those days did not vary much and consisted of the sort back and sides variety and I believe the cost of this service was sixpence. Immediately at the rear of his cottage once stood a Primitive Methodist capel, but I assume it closed when the new Chapel was built in the High Street in 1914 and no trace of this earlier building remains today.

CHAPTER SIXTY EIGHT

ALTHOUGH FARM HORSES were well fed and cared for they did not compare with the sleek highly groomed heavy horses that are seen at today's agricultural shows. Usually they spent their off work time turned out in the 'horse meadow' except in very bad weather when they would remain stabled. Anyone who has tried to groom a horse which is covered in mud or whose coat is wet will know that such time spent is time wasted. Also during the winter months these horses would have grown a winter coat and presented a very shaggy appearance. The self same animal in summer would take on the appearances of a sleek handsome beast,.no doubt giving the rise to the saying that 'a horse will grow fat on sunshine'.

Their tasks on the farm were many and varied but mainly involved pulling box carts, flat carts (fitted with rades) and the occasional four-wheeled wagon. Other horse drawn implements included seed drills, hoes, water carts and rakes. Ploughing, cultivating and pulling a binder had already become a job for the tractor. The head carter's day would start at about 6 am when the horses would be brought in from the paddock, fed and watered from a trough in the yard where they were able to drink before eating and again before going out to work, usually just after 8 am. Having fed and cleaned his charges, the Carter would return home for breakfast and then be back for work at 8 am when the rest of the staff would arrive. During harvest time when work would be taking place for several days at the same location, the carts and/or wagons would be left on site and the water cart made available to provide water for the horses. At the end of each day, usually well after dusk, the 'leaders' were able to ride home on the horses back. Makeshift reins were often made from binder twine. The seat was the most uncomfortable imaginable being on top of the 'pad' which had a deep wooden groove just where the rider had to sit. This groove was for the chain which supported the shafts of the vehicle, when the horse was connected to it. On his retirement, the head carter Chippy Taylor moved to a cottage on North Heath and together with this move came the inevitable change from Morlands Bitter (The Wheatsheaf) to Simonds (now Courage) beer at The Blue Boar.

When working away from the vicinity of their stables each horse would be provided with a nosebag containing crushed oats and wheat chaff, this to be consumed whilst the carter ate his own lunch usually consisting of bread and cheese often accompanied by a raw onion, washed down with a bottle of cold tea without milk or sugar.

Another unforgettable sight and smell was the heavy horses being shod at the Forge. The shoes were brought red hot direct from the Forge fire and placed on the hooves of the horse. Clouds of white acrid smoke rose from the horn of the hoof as the hot shoe was bedded into place and ensured a perfect fit. These were then cooled and attached to the hoof by nine nails in each hoof, four on the inner rim and five on the outer. This entire process was quite painless,but placed considerable strain on the body of the farrier. . Although there was always the odd "okkard owd sod" most of the horses were amiable gentle giants and totally unaware of their own strength. Anyone who has had dealings or connections with these animals cannot help but be thrilled to see their future secured if only for show or advertising purposes. Occasionally one can still see a pair of matched black horses with gleaming tack and often sporting black plumes on their heads, drawing an ornate hearse for a funeral. Likewise the same animals are still used to draw a wedding carriage, this adding an extra feature to the bride's special day.

The local farrier would travel to outlying farms to shoe the horses on site and he would make the shoes at the Forge, each set of shoes being made for the individual animal, the measurements of which would be known to the farrier.

One of the highlights of all agricultural shows must be the parade of heavy horses, particularly at the local Royal Berkshire Agricultural Show. My first recollection of Newbury Show was being taken by my father when it was held in the grounds of Shaw House. The entrance lodge and main gates were in the London road almost opposite St. Joseph's Church and the parkland covered the area between there and the house. There was of course no ring road or housing estate in existence at the time. This created a lasting memory and over the years apart from the War years and during my own National Service, I do not recall missing a single Show. The venues have changed several times since my first Show, and have taken place at Elcot Park, Henwick Manor,. Siege Cross Farm Thatcham, Whitelands Farm Donnington and finally to its permanent home at Chieveley, where it has become one of the Country's major two-day events.

SIXTY NINE

Several ponds were situated in the village, all of which served a very useful purpose prior to the main water supply being available. Water would be drawn from these ponds and transported to fields containing livestock. This was done by a horse-drawn watercart which would hold some two to three hundred gallons of water. This had to be filled by hand. The operator having backed the horse to the edge of the pond would use a bucket for filling purposes. A back aching job to be sure, particularly when he would have been balanced on a box or some other temporary staging, either in or at the edge of the pond and having to raise a full bucket some five feet in order to empty it into the cart.. This would then be carted to the field and tipped into a drinking trough by removing a wooden bung from the outlet at the base of the tank. Not an easy task as often a herd of thirst crazed cattle would be surrounding the trough in an effort to drink. Often in trying to replace the wooden bung in the outlet pipe, the operator received an unwelcome drenching.

During the summer months, especially in dry weather, it was often a full time job for a man and a horse to be at 'watercart' the whole time. Latterly Weaver's farm had a larger water container of some eight hundred gallons mounted on a four-wheeled chassis. This was drawn by a tractor and left in the field adjoining the drinking trough. The outlet was controlled by a valve and enabled the cattle to be watered on a daily basis. This particular method only took place after the coming of the mains water supply which allowed the tank to be filled by means of a hose pipe at the farm. Little did I realise in those days that in the coming years I would become a plumber and be personally responsible for laying many miles of underground water services to supply hundreds of water troughs in the area especially with the construction of the M4 motorway and the A34 alteration, both of which entailed a large amount of agricultural plumbing work.

The main ponds in the village were in the Square opposite the Wheatsheaf, filled in during the late 1920's., the Red Lion pond now filled in and used as a car park, Horsemoor pond which was situated in the garden of the house which takes its name "Ponders". This was filled in in the late 1930's when the house was purchased by Mrs. Charlesworth, a lady who bred and trained golden retriever gun-dogs. She adopted mostly masculine attire and with her short hair and deep speaking voice was often addressed as 'Sir'. Her dogs won many prizes and Crufts and other important Shows.

There is another pond at Downend which had a concrete wall built in front of it and in the 1940's, I well remember a large number of us local lads playing our version of ice-hockey on this pond by moonlight one very cold winter. This caused much concern to Mr. Marchant, who was the head gardener at Downend House and also a Special Constable. He broke the ice with a pickaxe to prevent further play. However a fall of rain followed by further frost enabled the sport to continue after only a few days.

CHAPTER SEVENTY

THE SIGHTS AND sounds of the countryside change with the seasons
as one year follows another. Most Januarys brought deep snows often
lasting for several weeks. February was often cold and wet hence
the saying 'February fill-dyke'. This was usually followed by a very
windy March bringing in the promise of spring with snowdrops in
bloom and rooks noisily pairing and starting to build their large
unruly nests. Often during March we experienced a very cold snap
. This was always known as 'blackthorn winter' as it coincided with
the first blooming of the blackthorn tree. Sunshine and showers
during April brought carpets of primroses in Bussock, Gidley and
Bradley Court Woods soon to be followed by a wonderful mass of
bluebells

Many a warm spell in April now brings out the ladies in their
summer frocks and the men hunt through the wardrobe for the shirts
and shorts packed away last autumn. 'Ne'er cast a clout 'til May be
out' is a well known old saying. I have never been able to find out
whether this refers to the month of May or the blossom on the May
tree.

April and May sees the flowering of the hawthorn, wild cherry,
sloe, May and many other native trees, whilst the road side verges

in the countryside are awash with, campion, coltsfoot, wild clematis or travellers joy and other wild flowers. With the introduction of the tractor mounted mechanical hedge trimmer, most hedges are cut annually and regrettably many of the wild flower species have disappeared. Conversley however, with the proliferation of garden centres many exotic shrubs and flowering trees have become available which means that many gardens now boast a feast of spring colour. While magnolias and lilac flourish on the local mainly chalk sub-soil it does not please the lime hating plants of the azalea, rhododendron and camelia family. The different shades of green foliage covering the treees in the early spring make it very difficult to image the same trees stark and bare against a winter sky just a few months previously. Still to come are the magnificent candle-type blossoms of the horse chestnut which eventually give a crop of conkers in the autumn. In May and June the gardens begin to come into their own, with tall majestic hollyhocks and delphiniums, foxgloves, sweetpeas, roses and later, dahlias, chrysanthemums and Michaelmas daisies. Some of these were of course the old traditional cottage garden flowers.

The fronts of several houses in the village are adorned with many old types of rambler rose and clematis and present a stunning display during the summer season.

Today, some roadside verges are still a mass of white flowered cowparsley. Years back, the predominant colour of fields planted with cereal crops would go from bright yellow (charlock) to bright red (poppies) and then to blue (thistle and cornflower). Today modern spraying has almost eliminated these wild flowers as weeds.

Another memory from the summer of 1943 was when on several consecutive late evenings, and very dark, there were a large number of fireflies in the vicinity of Church Farm, this being the only time I have ever seen these remarkable insects.

In the days of the smaller farm, the owner would have livestock and have a meadow from which hay was produced to feed cattle during the winter months. These meadows would contain a vast mixture of wild flowers and the resulting hay, when properly made, had a wonderful perfume. Another wild flower, the golden buttercup was prolific during the early spring but apart from its beautiful colour served no useful purpose whatever.

Another yellow flower which again is rampant is the dandelion. This flower however had at least one important use as the flower heads were picked by the bucketful and boiled to become the main ingredient of home made dandelion wine (one of the most potent beverages known to man). This wine is reputed to improve with age but no proof of this claim could be discovered as the wine made by my Grandmother, many gallons each year, had always been consumed within a few weeks of being produced.

St,. George's Day was always reckoned to be the day on which to pick the dandelions after which it would be several weeks before the stains finally disappeared from the hands of the pickers.

Cowslips were another meadow flower used extensively in the making of home made wine and were much more abundant than they seem to be today. A good many natural ingredients were used for home wine making, including elder flowers, elder berries (they make a very good cough syrup) black currants, white currants, red currants, damsons, sloes, pea pods, wheat, parsnip and other root crops. Home made cider was another popular brew, mostly referred to as 'scrumpy' and usually extremely potent.

CHAPTER SEVENTY ONE

THE TRADITIONAL AGRICULTURAL tasks followed each other year by year, ploughing, cultivating, sowing, haymaking, hoeing and harvest with each year differing from its predecessor due to the vagaries of our climate. However, crops planted late due to wet conditions usually had a habit of catching up as the season progressed. Wet weather had a much more disastrous effect on crops at the end of the season, mainly due to the fact that the harvest took much longer to complete because of the intensive labour content. Persistent rain during September would often soak the 'stooks' which were still standing in the fields causing the grain to 'grow out' rendering it quite unusable even as poultry or animal feed.

This was doubly disappointing to the poor farmer, who having lost his crop, would then have to pick up the ruined stooks and dispose of them in order to allow ploughing to commence in readiness for planting the next year's crop.

As the season progressed so the bounty of the hedgerow became available in the form of nuts and berries, blackberries being gathered in large quantities and used in the making of jams and jellies. Also in the cattle meadows, mushrooms were usually plentiful during the months of September and October. Another memorable sight on a misty autumn evening as dusk was falling would be the white barn owl flying silently across the fields and hovering before dropping on some unsuspecting field mouse or vole.

The little owl or 'willy' owl as it was known was also found in large numbers and one would often lie in bed at night and listen to its seemingly unending mournful cry, possibly not regarded as a mournful cry to another little owl. Later still with the approach of Christmas, many of the local holly trees would seem mysteriously to lose some of their stature, especially if well covered with crimson berries.

Unlike some of the neighbouring villages I cannot recall mistletoe growing on any trees in the village.

Many of the old familiar village sounds have gone for ever, the steady clip-clop of the heavy horse drawing a loaded cart up the High Street, the heart-rending all night bellowing of a cow whose calf had just been taken away from her to be weaned. This calf would then be fed and raised if a heifer or probably packed off to market if a bull-calf. Another unforgettable country sound was the scream of a love-lorn vixen in search of a mate which could often be heard on a moonlight January night. At least the local poultry farmer would know that her particular plans on that night had nothing to do with his chickens. Another well known sound which depended on the type of weather and the direction of the wind was the noise of a train whistle as it approached Hermitage Station. This was regarded to be a sure sign of rain. Farmer John Weaver would often stand at the corner of Church Lane and watch the rooks as they perched on the weather vane at the top of the Church tower. Their particular antics would then allow him to decide the programme of work for his staff that day and perhaps whether to start haymaking or harvest. If the rooks flew from the weather vane in a direct line then he would be assured that fine weather would be forthcoming.

People either singly, in pairs, groups or families could on summer evenings be seen walking, enjoying the delights of the countryside. Perhaps the lack of a motor cars contributed to this way of life but today's rush and tear approach leaves many folk who live in the village totally unaware of the surrounding countryside and the pleasures that it has to offer. Unfortunately for some, the only sight of a badger, rabbit or fox is as a corpse at the side of the road viewed from a passing car.

CHAPTER SEVENTY TWO

M<small>Y MANY REMINISCENCES</small> in connection with the game of cricket would in themselves be sufficient to fill a book. The following items are a few of the incidents which took place during a playing career spanning some thirty years. This started in the late 1930's at a time when my father was playing for Chieveley and I would be always there hoping that Chieveley or their opponents would be a man short and allow me to play, even if it meant batting at number eleven and being treated to some easy bowling by the opposing team. One early recollection was a game against Marlston Cricket Club on the ground which is now the playing field of Brockhurst School. Being some sixteen years old and having been batting reasonably well, Harry Booker, the Captain, took me in with him to open the batting. The opposing bowler for Marlston sent me the first ball of the match. With a lunge down the wicket I hit it for a towering six over a group of trees which stood close to the boundary. Next I saw the Captain striding down the wicket, but instead of offering the expected congratulations he called me everything under the sun for not taking time to play myself in. How many runs I made I cannot remember but recall Harry failing to score in that particular game.

During the mid 1940's Chieveley were playing an away game against the RAF personnel at Welford Camp . The pitch was right out in the middle of the airfield and I remember there was not even a chair to sit on let alone a pavilion of any sort. This had the effect of making the ground appear huge. Batting at number three or four I was at the wicket with Ted Bullock. He was an excellent bat and very strong on the off side. Off one ball he hit a hard drive past extra cover and we set off between the wickets. Being considerably more agile in those days I was fairly fast between the wickets. Ted had run three runs and on grounding his bat looked over his shoulder to see if I was coming for a fourth run. To his great consternation, he could not see me as having run four runs to his three I was standing behind him. Fortunately the ball had crossed the boundary line so both wickets remained intact. As a point of law I have often pondered what the umpire's decision would have been if the ball had been returned from inside the boundary and the wicket broken at the opposite end to the one where we both stood.

During Sid Leach's time as Captain we were playing an away match at Peasemore. The wicket at that time consisted of a strip of coconut matting, the edges of which were slightly lower than the surrounding turf. Often a wily bowler would pitch a delivery on the edge of the mat, causing the ball to break back towards the batsman at an alarming rate. Along this time in the late 1940's and early 50's very few outfields were mown. Correspondingly scores were much lower than those of today, sixty or seventy runs often being a winning score. Mr. Gerald Palmer was at that time, President of Chieveley Cricket Club and for some years had generously donated a new bat to any member who managed to score fifty runs. On one particular day at Peasemore I achieved the feat and after the applause had died down faced the next ball. Feeling very pleased with myself, I took an almighty swing at it and was caught just inside the long leg boundary. On my arrival back at the pavilion I was promptly informed that the applause had been premature and that in fact I had only scored forty nine. As a teenager I had probably not learned many expletives but did the best I could.

Jack Winter was a gifted all-round sportsman and a notable

cricketer. Not a very tall man, he was a very accurate fast bowler and prolific wicket taker. In my own time as Captain, Jack was often encouraged to bowl unchanged during an entire innings. As a batsman he was a very hard hitter of the ball, always straight or on the off side, seldom if ever scoring runs on the leg side. Playing a game against Newbury second X1 he scored the very first century on the Northcroft ground, knocking thirty two runs off one over. Sometimes when batting together we would have a small bet as to who could run the other out. This caused great confusion to the fielding side and runs were often taken by stopping the ball in the block hole or taking byes to the wicket keeper, usually with the non-striking batsman backing up and calling for the run as soon as the bowler had released the ball. An amazing number of runs were scored in this fashion.

Chieveley Cricket Club played quite a few games against Armed Forces teams. At the beginning of the war I remember playing against an RAF side at Wyld Court aerodrome at Hampstead Norris. With the building of Hermitage camp some two years later, the turf from the wicket at Wyld Court was taken up and relaid at Hermitage Camp on the new playing field, then sited alongside the road to Priors Court. After the war years I played many games on this pitch, both for Chieveley and also for the Camp Staff team during the time I was carrying out the plumbing contract there. Some years later this same turf was again moved and relaid in its existing position in the Camp in conjuction with the major building works which took place. I played one game on this ground and have therefore played on the same wicket in three different places.

For several years, I also played for Newbury Wednesday Cricket Club, which as the name suggests played their games mid-week. A game at Queen Anne's School Caversham was played on a pitch where the outfield and adjoining playing field had a considerable slope and after retrieving a big hit, I remember telling the tale that the ball went so far it took three throws to return it to the wicket.

Bill Coster was fielding at cover point in a game against Savernake Forest C.C. Being unable to bend down quickly enough to pick up a fierce off drive, he put his legs together and saved a certain four by stopping the ball with his shins. The noise was such that everyone expected broken bones, but fortunately only bruising occurred.

However speaking to him just a few days ago, i.e., some forty years later, he assured me that the marks were still visible.

It was not unusual in village matches for teams to turn up without an umpire. This task would then be undertaken by various members of the batting side. In a match at Donnington, whilst umpiring at the bowler's end, the batsman was struck on the pad immediately in front of the stumps, I instantly appealed in a loud voice for lbw. Fortunately the bowler did the same and I had no option but to give him out. My later years were spent playing cricket at Highclere, which was then one of the best grounds in the district. We played an away game against Goring C.C. Our Vicar, the Reverend Brian Goodrich had a son who was Captain and opening bat for Marlborough College. At my suggestion he was included in the Highclere team on that day. Winning the toss we elected to bat, but as the home team were a man short I offered to field as a substitute. Before he had scored a run, the Vicar's son played a wonderful square drive in the direction of point, where I was fielding. Diving full length in an attempt to stop the ball, I was astonished to find that it had stuck in my hand and he was out for a duck. I was not the most popular player in the side, especially since I had to drive the unfortunate batsman home after the game. However we did win that particular match. Matches between Highclere CC and Newbury CC were always very competitive affairs. One Sunday afternoon Highclere had batted first and made a fairly good score. After declaring at tea time, the Newbury openers John Spencer and John Wyatt came to the wicket and settled in and built a large opening partnership. It just so happened that I had a plastic snake in my pocket which I dropped on the ground close to the square leg umpire at the end of the over. At the beginning of the next over the batsman noticed the reptile and he set about 'killing' it with his bat. At this point I casually walked across and put the corpse back into my pocket. The outcome of the event being that the unfortunate batsman, John Wyatt had lost his concentration and was bowled by the very next bowl. This was before the word "sledging" was invented. Highclere ran out winners on the day but I often wonder what the result would have been had we not been assisted by the 'snake' which after the match was returned to my boys' toy box.

Many cricket grounds which I recall playing on with Chieveley have now gone. One of my first memories was playing against Westwood CC , Newbury. Their ground was in Boundary Road on a site now occupied by blocks of flats near the Racecourse. Wessex CC also in Newbury played on a ground adjoining the old Bath Road which is now a housing site. During the winter months this ground was home to Reading A Football Club. One summer whilst a new stand was being built for the forthcoming football season, Jack Winter hit a six and made a large hole in the asbestos roof of the new building just a few days after it had been put in place. Another ground that has long since returned to agricultural use was that of Inholmes CC at Lambourn Woodlands. Fortunately the grounds at Priors Court and Marlston are still used as playing fields.

The demise of sports fields has also been suffered by several football pitches on which we played as youngsters. Eastfield Old Boys played on a pitch at the rear of Newbury Hospital in the Andover Road on a ground known as the City Playground. We changed in a room at the Red House pub in Argyle Road, that area of Newbury always being known as The City. Another Newbury pub, the Drummers Arms in Northcroft Lane was used as a changing room for football played on a pitch now the home of Newbury Hockey Club.

CHAPTER SEVENTY THREE

THE RURAL PURSUITS which afforded so much pleasure to my generation, together with our football, cricket and other sports have now given way to the delights of the mobile telephone with its associated text messages, I-Pods, videos and personal computers. Violence seems to be an everyday part of today's existence, gone are the days when people left doors and windows unlocked while away from the premises. Bolts, bars and electronic devices have all regrettably added to the disappearance of the community spirit of village life.. Having been born, raised, educated and subsequently brought up my own family in Chieveley I have a strong feeling of affinity with the village. Fortunately many of the old familiar faces are still with us and while the surroundings have undergone some changes a few of the old and treasured memories and village traditions remain. The village has few redeeming characteristics. True it boasts an old Church, parts of which are from Norman times, and some fine old houses, other than these there are not many features of outstanding significance.

During its history no major battles have taken place in the near vicinity. It has never had a castle or a stately home or any particularly famous inhabitants. It has neither lake nor river, no mountain or even a hill of any size. The railway never came and even the Oxford road, the A34 Preston to Winchester trunk road, passed by to the east. It has never been home to any form of major industry other than agriculture which was common to most villages in the land. Yet, despite the lack of these attributes, it is still a delightful village and one which I hope to remain in contact with until the end of my days, after which perhaps I will join my ancestors who have been associated with the village for many generations. The Churchyard holds memorials to Great Grandmother Barratt (North side of the tower), my Grandparents and Parents, together with a large number of Aunts and Uncles of the Leach family. .

CHAPTER SEVENTY FOUR

MY EARLY ARMY Cadet training went some way to preparing me for National Service which came just four years after my exploits at Welford Base. On obtaining the grand old age of eighteen I received a very nice letter from King George VI requesting the pleasure of my company at Parsons Barracks Aldershot on the 4th November 1948 for which he kindly enclosed a travel warrant. I recall also that in the small print, it did mention the fact that if I did not avail myself of this generous offer - they would come and get me. After two weeks at this reception camp the grounds of which adjoined Aldershot Town Football Club, I had been kitted out in denims, the trousers of which had been designed for a person some six inches shorter in the leg than myself and given no less than three haircuts. I, together with some two hundred like individuals, was moved to Salamanca Barracks also in Aldershot (long since demolished and now the site of a Police Station). After some three months of basic training I had been transformed from a plumber to a Clerk/Typist with the RAOC (Royal Army Ordnance Corps now the Royal Logisitics Corps). Also from being a crack shot with a catapult to a first class shot with a

Lee Enfield .300 rifle and a Bren gun but being attached to a Corps as opposed to an Infantry Regiment, the Cross-Rifles insignia of a marksman were not worn. I was most upset.

Being afflicted with slightly fallen arches and a tendency to turn my toes in,and still do, I obtained a 'chitty' from the MO and was "excused boots". As one cannot wear FMSO (Full Service Marching Order) with shoes I was unfortunately unable to take part in the square bashing and route marches being 'enjoyed' by the remainder of the platoon. Again I was most upset. After completing my training in Aldershot I was posted to Weedon in Northamptonshire. This camp had been the home of the Army Roughriders School which had trained most of the Army Cavalry horses in earlier times. During my stay there it was a small arms depot responsible for distribution of arms to our forces worlwide. This posting allowed weekend visits home and all went well until once again His Majesty intervened and I was sent to Malaya.

The outward journey was from Southampton on a vessel named "Empire Ken" where together with several hundred others I was accommodated some distance below the water line in canvas bunks three high and more than a little cramped. The outward trip took twenty eight days with a few brief hours ashore at Port Said and again in Colombo, Ceylon, (now Sri Lanka). On arrival in Singapore a few days were spent in a transit camp, the same Barracks that only a few weeks later were to be home to the writer Leslie Thomas, who used his experience as a National Serviceman to write his best seller "The Virgin Soldiers" and several related books to follow. Reading his books brings back many memories of that part of the world. My remaining Army career was spent in Johore, Malaya at an ex-Ghurka Barracks built by the Japanese during the second World War. This unit was number 221 Vehicle Battalion and was responsible for the supply of vehicles, tanks and spares to the whole of Malaya. This was during the time that the Chinese Communists were very active. Besides working during the day, each fourth night would be spent on armed guard at one or other of the various vehicle parks or kit stores in an attempt to prevent looting and theft. Whilst never actively called upon to fire a weapon in anger, the kit stores which was my daily place of work was broken into one night and acting on a tip-off, the Ghurkas shot dead several of the Chinese bandits who were attempting to steal vehicle parts.

My own particular National Service release group number was 146 and I left Singapore in April 1950 on the troop ship "Orbita". This was to be her last trip before going to the breakers and in the middle of the Indian Ocean some eight days from Singapore and another eight from Colombo she managed to lose one of her three propellers. This resulted in the trip home taking thirty one days. However, I was slightly more fortunate than Leslie Thomas, who had a release group number of about 150, each group number being some two weeks apart. All those of his group and above had an additional six months added to the length of their National Service. Our boat eventually arrived in Liverpool in the middle of a very wet May night from whence we were taken by train to Aldershot for 'demob' and home to Chieveley in time for the beginning of the cricket season.

During my time away from home I longed to be back with the friends made at school, I longed to be back on the cricket field or to be standing in that particularly muddy patch between the goal posts, except at the end of the season when that self same patch of earth took on the aspect and texture of concrete. As the years progressed I began to realise that my spell of National Service was the best thing that could possibly have happened to me, having given me a wealth of memories of places that I probably would never have visited, and a sense of comradeship, loyalty and trust which is often sadly lacking in the youth of today.

CHAPTER SEVENTY FIVE

M Y WORKING LIFE resumed for Messrs. E Lipscomb & Sons of Oxford Street, Newbury where I continued my work as a plumber for approximately eighteen months, before setting up my own business which I operated from a workshop in Manor Lane, Chieveley. This was brought about mainly by being asked to carry out odd plumbing jobs for friends at weekends. However this soon became more than I could cope with and the decision was made to branch out on my own. The business was formed under the rather grand title of "Martin of Chieveley" and carried on until my retirement in 1995 (45 years).

One of my first contracts was for Mr. Ralph Burgess, Builder and Undertaker of Hermitage. He was at that time carrying out work in connection with a grant-scheme conversion on many cottages belonging to the Yattendon Estate. This work involved fitting a Rayburn cooker/water heater with hot and cold water storage tanks and all connected with galvanized steel pipework, fitting bath, basin, w.c., and kitchen sink with all hot and cold connections, wastes and overflows. The labour charge for each house varied slightly due to the nature of the building and was between £25 and £35 per house. (

Business ledgers carrying these figures are still in my possession).

Needless to say no vast profits were made from such a venture, but working for Ralph Burgess did make one huge change in my life and soon I was to marry Joyce, his younger daughter. We did, for reasons of living in adjoining villages, know each other by sight and by taking part in the odd game of tennis in Chieveley, when I was also at that time, Groundsman at the Recreation Centre. Joyce was working in London, but as our friendship developed, returned home to live and work for the Agricultural Research Council at Compton. We were married in Hermitage Church on 15th June 1957 and after a reasonably small reception set off on our honeymoon in a newly acquired Ford Escort van, for a secret destination known only to myself.

Stratford on Avon had been my choice, having thought at the time that if it was good enough for the other William, it would be good enough for me. In late afternoon on a gloriously hot sunny day, we enquired at almost every hotel for a room, only to be told "Sorry we're full, there's a Shakespeare Festival on". One kind soul suggested we try Henley in Arden. This we attempted but with the same results. We had no option but to press on, and drove through the centre of Birmingham at around 6 pm with the sky an inky black preceding a torrential thunder storm. - no motorways or ring roads in those days. Becoming increasingly concerned as to where our first night would be spent, we eventually arrived at the world famous honeymoon centre of Walsall and booked into the George Hotel. We were convinced that the Hotel staff, in those days anyway, could recognise a newly-wed couple from a mile off, so in flippant mood I asked the lady at the reception desk if she had a double room with a sea view. This went down like the proverbial lead balloon. However they did us proud and the next morning after an excellent dinner, bed and breakfast, I was presented with the bill which was for seventeen shillings and sixpence each (or £1. 75 for both of us)

This considerable expense caused us to have a rethink regarding our financial resources. We had pooled every penny before the wedding and between us had amassed the princely sum of almost £60. It was doubtful that this was going to last the whole two weeks of the honeymoon. However, casting all discretion to the wind we pressed on with our mini-tour of England. This took us to Blackpool, Grasmere and Pooley Bridge in the Lake District, Southport, York and Cambridge, finally arriving home two days early and stoney broke.

Ralph Burgess and Joyce's brother Jack had built a new bungalow for us to move into along the Hampstead Norris road and although the inside was almost complete the garden area outside was reminiscent of the Somme in World War One. We were very pleased for all the hard work they had carried out to have the place ready for occupation, and I still have our rent book showing the rent at ten shillings per week (50p). In the weeks and months to come I removed many large trees with the aid of a hand operated winch borrowed from Messrs. Barlow & Sons, and laid paths and with the help of my father something resembling a garden eventually materialised.

A second-hand bedroom suite and a couple of armchairs formed the total sum of the furniture, whilst in the kitchen we had a tea trolley on wheels, and two kitchen chairs. After a meal, instead of clearing the table/trolley, it was easier to remain seated and push the trolley aside. As the wedding had not been a large affair, we had not been inundated with presents, in fact we had no cutlery and had I not thoughtfully collected two each of these items from the junk room at the Chequers Hotel whilst working there, it would have made meal times a bit awkward.

Gradually we managed to furnish the bungalow and made things generally more comfortable, although I seem to remember that the back bedroom always resembled a tip. Subsequently, the site opposite my workshop in Chieveley became available, this I purchased and submitted plans for a house. Another plan also came into being with the arrival of Stephen John in April 1959, at which time Joyce gave up work at Compton and took over running the office side of the business as by this time I was employing staff, which involved PAYE tax forms, accounts, balance sheets and so forth.

In the spring of 1960 the house at Chieveley called "Corner House" was finished and the move from Hermitage completed with the aid of a Ford van and many journeys. Some two years after our move to Chieveley, the family was increased by the arrival of twins, Neil and Gary . This made for a lot of work especially before the advent of the disposable nappy. Lead pipe joints were not all I became expert at wiping. Soon they were all three off to my own seat of learning, Chieveley School, from there on to Compton and Newbury Grammar School . The twins both joined the Army as juniors at sixteen years. When I tell my grandchildren that Chieveley was the only school I attended, they ask the question "But you must have gone somewhere else when you reached fourteen?" to which I reply "Yes I did - out to work".

CHAPTER SEVENTY SIX

CHANGES WERE TAKING place in the plumbing trade at this time, with copper pipe and cylinders replacing the old fashioned galvanised pipes and tanks. Asbestos cement and latterly fibreglass cold water storage tanks became the vogue and plastic pipe the favoured material for underground services, plastic also being used for soil waste and overflow pipes. We also specialised in converting Rayburn cookers to oil and many dozens were adapted from solid fuel. Working for several different main contractors, we carried out plumbing and maintenance work at various military installations including Greenham Common, Welford Camp, Thatcham Depot and Hermitage Camp.

Maintenance work was also undertaken to properties in the local area for the Newbury Rural District Council, who at that time owned all the housing stock, now the responsibility of Sovereign Housing.

Newbury RDC was also responsible for the water supply to the area and we carried out mains tapping and services to new properties both in the Chieveley and Wickham areas. We carried out the tapping and services to all of the new properties on the North side of Graces

Lane. This entailed the use of a pick and shovel and digging down to expose the main, usually some three to four feet, tapping the main and driving a service under the road, terminating in a stopcock at the boundary of the new site. My records show that one particular job was undertaken for the sum of £14 16s 10p. This was for two men working one day and materials. including the provision of asphalt to reinstate the road surface. Such a job carried out today would involve partial road closure, the use of traffic lights, mechanical excavators and so on. From past experience the use of a mechanical digger involves a) the driver and b) several paid spectators and in no way reduces the time taken to complete the work. The cost today would perhaps be somewhat in excess of the above fee.

By this time the workforce had increased to five or six men and we had three vans on the road. .Another customer who provided a large amount of work was S W Brown & Sons of Peasemore, especially at their Gidley Farm, which housed an intensive pig-breeding and rearing unit. Many hundreds of thousands of pigs were bred there and as all were automatically fed and watered, miles of pipework was fitted for this purpose. Sadly with the decline in the pig industry, this unit is no more. At this time in conjunction with S.W.Brown and the Pig Improvement Company at Checkendon, Oxfordshire, we carried out a large amount of experimental work regarding methods of feeding and watering. Many of the innovations which we perfected at Gidley were then taken up by the PIC, to be used worldwide, regrettably with no financial gain to ourselves.

Several apprentices were taken on by "Martin of Chieveley" and today Michael Calloway,of Chieveley, and Dennis Bune of Cold Ash now operate their own businesses, hopefully aided by a few tips gained from their time with me.

Oil fired heating became very popular and provided a great deal of work. Over the years I had become a member of The Worshipful Company of Plumbers. The National Federation of Building Trades Employers. The National Federation of Plumbing and Domestic Heating Engineers and an appointed installer for Shell and BP and Don oil burners. It was impossible to attend all meetings of the above Federations but I gave my support as and when I could.

Another of my main customers was the Yattendon Estates. They owned in excess of three hundred houses and numerous farms and in later years most of my time was spent there. During the early 1970's I was elected to the Chieveley Parish Council and after three years became Chairman (not 'Chair' a title used today and which I strongly detest). This post I held for fifteen years at the end of which time I was presented with an inscribed tankard by my fellow members of the Council.

Subsequently I moved to Hermitage, which has been my home ever since and where I am only 300 yards outside Chieveley Parish boundary.

CHAPTER SEVENTY SEVEN

ON MY RETURN to 'civvy street' my next objective was to obtain some means of transport. My first car was a Morris 8 Series E and was purchased with the help of my parents who although they could ill afford the cost of a car, were determined that I would not have the alternative, a motorcycle, on which they were convinced my life would be drastically shortened.

Again, after leaving the Army, the years of the early 1950's saw Chieveley with a very successful football team of which I was proud to be a member,. The Cricket Team also flourished, mainly due our new ground at the Recreation Centre and the excellent facilities on offer. Our team also played in and won several evening 'knockout' cup competitions. At this time the new tennis courts were constructed, now increased from two to four. Because I played a great deal of cricket, very little time was left for tennis , although it was very enjoyable. Playing with Reg Goodchild as a partner in the Newbury knockout competition, we were drawn against Basil Hutchins and his partner. They had competed at Wimbledon the week previous to our meeting. This took place at Chieveley one Sunday morning and although I have no recollection of the final score, I seem to recall that we were very poor runners-up.

The Chieveley Badminton Club was formed soon after the building of the new hall. Our team would often visit other clubs for friendly matches my favourite venue being the old Corn Exchange in Newbury which housed four courts and provided excellent entertainment .

Another priority was to master the art of ball-room dancing which, whilst being most enjoyable, was the main method of meeting the opposite sex,. also with the added attraction of a motor car in which to transport one's dancing partner home from the dance. Having become reasonably proficient a the noble art, together with Reg Goodchild we managed to cover many thousands of miles visiting most of the dance halls, both large and small from the Lyceum in the Strand,and Hammersmith Palais in London ,to Brightwalton and Leckampstead village halls. The Corn Exchange Newbury hosted weekly dances often bringing in the Big Bands of the day, namely Harry Gold and his Pieces of Eight, Cyril Stapleton, Ted Heath, Jack Parnell etc at which four to five hundred dancers would be present. Then, the whole floor was an area for dancing with seats round the perimeter wall. Another popular venue for dances was The Plaza Ballroom, now the offices of Dreweatt Neate.

If I only had a pound for every mile covered on the dance floor I would now be living a life of luxury, albeit with a few complaints from an ageing pair of knees. My dancing exploits led me to become part of the France Belk Pantomime team in Newbury and for many years the Studio in Station Approach and the Corn Exchange stage would be the place I could often be found. Having returned to my old employer at the end of my army service my boss's brother Ted was the then Stage Manager to the Newbury Operatic Society and I became involved as a member of the Stage Crew. Next I joined the Society as a dancer and then as a singer. This all started in 1950 and since that time have taken part in many musical stage shows. I have many wonderful memories of past shows and the fun which we all had on and off the stage.

Also when first leaving the Army I joined the Royal County Operatic Society who were performing Noel Coward's "Bitter Sweet" at the Palace Theatre, Reading, long since demolished. Also, with Miss Iris Brooks the Newbury Dancing Teacher, I took part in a "Festival of Dance" held in the Empress Hall, Earls Court, London. This programme included all types of dancing, our particular item being an Elizabethan 'Galliard'.. Appearing on the same bill was Bill Hailey and the Comets, the Ted Heath Band and Victor Sylvester and His Ballroom Orchestra. I well remember Iris Brooks introducing Eric Rowe a fellow dancer, and myself to Victor. We were marched by Iris across the front of the stage to where Victor was conducting the Orchestra before a crowd of some four to five hundred dancers. The introductions were made and a long chat ensued and as the old saying goes 'the band played on'. We were to meet on several occasions after this and I still feel that his style of music will remain the finest possible tempo to dance to. This was probably because he himself had been a world champion ballroom dancer before forming his Orchestra, later to be conducted by his son Victor Junior.

My own sporting activities carried on apace but football finished abruptly when at the age of twenty seven I injured my elbow whilst playing in goal at Frilsham one cold snowy day. This entailed some eight weeks off work. Being self-employed I had no wage, except for a cheque from the Berks and Bucks Football Benevolent Association for £12, I realised that I could no longer risk any further football injuries. Much time was spent playing cricket at weekends and evenings and occasionally tennis. Joyce however was a very good tennis player and played in several competitions.

Towards the middle of the 1960's the interest in the Chieveley Cricket Club waned and the Club eventually folded. I was very lucky then to play for Highclere at the Whiteoak Ground at the Castle, when Henry, Lord Porchester (later Lord Carnarvon) was playing. During his representative games the Club members were always in attendance and we met many of the famous Cricketers who were taking part,. the special ones being Dennis Compton, the Bedser twins, Colin Ingleby-McKenzie and my own cricketing hero, Australian, Keith Miller. With the demise of the Highclere Village Cricket Team, my cricketing career came to an end in my late forties.

CHAPTER SEVENTY EIGHT

HORSES BECAME A passion and for the next fifteen years or so, took up every spare hour and most of my spare cash. My three sons had become interested in riding because their cousin Lynn owned a pony at Hermitage. This led to their attending Falkland Riding School which was owned by Mr. Henry Hall . Joyce also started riding there and rode a gentle thoroughbred mare by the name of Goldie. This animal unfortunately died giving birth to a foal and was in fact the only horse Joyce ever rode. During the time the rest of the family was riding, I sat around waiting for the lesson to finish. One day Henry Hall, together with Joyce contrived to get me on to the back of a horse. This however, was an animal named Tonto, a large skewbald beast that Henry's son David had ridden in showjumping and cross country events. Full of oats and raring to go this evil monster promptly took off with a terrified novice on board, much to the delight of the organisers of the conspiracy. It seemed as if we had galloped several miles before he decided to slow down and eventually we managed to get back to the stables in one piece.

From that day on I was completely hooked and soon became

proficient enough to ride the same animal on a regular basis. Sons Stephen and Gary lost interest in riding, but Neil was very keen and soon we were the proud owners of a New Forest pony by the name of Champ, and so began the three hundred and sixty five days a year hobby of horse owning. Having our own horse provided another problem. A young rider had to be accompanied when riding out which meant that poor old Dad was then mounted on a bicycle or ran on foot in a vain attempt to keep up. Next came the need for transporting the said horse to local shows, which involved the purchase of a Rice trailer. This in turn meant buying a larger car to tow the thing.

At about this time I was working at an equestrian establishment locally converting a Rayburn cooker to oil. The topic of riding came up and the eventual outcome was that the owner of the farm had his conversion carried out for free and I became the owner of a 16'2 hh bay gelding by the name of 'Sam Browne'. He was a very sad looking character having been turned out for a very long time. His feet had the appearance of frying pans and both mane and tail were long, matted and full of burrs. Geoff Sampson the farrier sorted out the feet and after many hours of grooming, lots of food and tender loving care the old chap took on a completely new lease of life.

Sam Browne soon taught me how to ride and turned out to be the perfect schoolmaster. In no time at all, we were jumping hedges fences and ditches and I began to think I could ride. These thoughts however, came to an abrupt halt on our first days hunting together. The meet was the Vine & Craven Hunt at Walter Smith's Elm Grove Farm, Downend. It is impossible to describe the change which came over that horse as soon as he joined the rest of the field. He was obviously an experienced hunter and became so full of himself that I had great difficulty in controlling him. In fact most of the time he was the one in charge.

Local show jumping was attempted but soon given up as a bad job as I seemed to spend as much time lying on the ground as I did sitting on the horse. There is an old saying that you never ever fall off your horse, you are always "thrown". It may sound much nicer but is still just as painful.

Whilst working for Roddy Armitage, the National Hunt trainer at East Ilsley, he had a 17.2hh racehorse looking for a good home on

retirement from racing. This horse was called Fitzcard and was owned
by Mr. Bill Whitbread a member of the brewing family and a well
known figure in National Hunt racing. This old horse had won many
races during his career and loved jumping hedges and rails, ditches
being quite a different matter. He covered the ground at an amazing
speed but was totally impossible to stop. We had many exciting days
hunting together. Soon after Fitzcard I purchased a three-quarter bred
Irish mare. She proved an excellent hunter and one of her outstanding
features being that should I, whilst out hunting, decide to stop for a
drink, she would stand outside the pub patiently awaiting my return
without being tethered. Several other thoroughbreds followed from
various racing sources, my last being a jet-black 17.3hh gelding
called 'Ebony Lad' (Ebbo). He also had enjoyed a successful career
in racing and had been at one time the biggest horse in training. He
was perfect in both manners and performance and took to hunting
like a duck to water.

The bond between horse and rider, especially if one looks after the
horse, is amazingly strong and to part with such a close companion
when the time comes, is a heart rending experience. In the early
days several ponies came and went, as Neil grew. Also I bred some
Welsh Section A ponies which were taken to local shows, winning
some novice classes. My connection with horses was only possible
by the kindness of the owners of Chieveley Manor. Firstly Mr. and
Mrs. David Rolt, then Mr. and Mrs. Simon Courtauld and lastly Mr.
and Mrs. Christopher Spence, all of whom allowed me to stable my
horses and use the paddocks. Mr. and Mrs. Spence have now turned
the yard into a first class modern Stud and have had considerable
success with their home bred horses.

There can be few experiences more exhilarating than to be astride
a fit thoroughbred horse at full gallop, especially on a nice day and
on good going, and with a post and rail fence or hedge looming up
immediately ahead. In my own case most of my riding was spent
fox hunting during the winter months and exercising horses early
mornings, in order to be home again in time to start work. In the
winter months this would be in the dark often in the freezing cold
or pouring rain. Much of the time during the summer, horses are
"turned out" with shoes removed and have a well earned rest.

CHAPTER SEVENTY NINE

In the late 1980's several friends suggested I take up the game of bowls. This I did, joining Hungerford Bowls Club enjoying many years of outdoor bowling. Since that time I have played for Harwell Bowls Club and most summers tour with the Berkshire Masonic Bowling association, travelling to various parts of Britain.

When first moving into Corner House, my father helped me to get the garden into some sort of order and I remember how pleased he was when I won my first classes at Chieveley Horticultural Show, for tomatoes and onions. Sadly he developed leukemia and after a protracted illness died on 9th March 1967 aged 77. My mother remarried and moved to London where she also died on the 9th March 1999 at the age of 93.

Joyce and I had been married for thirty six years when tragically cancer struck and after a relatively short illness she passed away on the 15th June 1993 on the anniversary of our wedding day. Having worked so hard and enjoyed life together we had been planning all the things we would do on my retirement. Wonderful memories remain and also a supportive and loving family, but I also recall the nagging doubt of 'where do I go from here?'

Having remained a member of Newbury Operatic Society, at a rehearsal I met with Jill (Buxey). Jill had been a widow for some five years and after reminiscing over past shows, we arranged some day trips out when we discovered we had many interests in common, gardening, singing, dancing, travel etc.

The friendship blossomed and we were married at Chieveley by Rev.Colin Scott-Dempster on 12th March 1994. We had a wonderful day surrounded by family and friends and spent our honeymoon in Guernsey. We now had five children between us with Jill's daughter Kate and son Adam, but all of them had left home some years prior to our wedding which left us free to enjoy ourselves. Soon after this I retired and we were able to do many things which years ago would have been but dreams. That as the saying goes , is another story.

In the late 1970's several friends, in particular Dick Cann, Lou Watts and my brother in law Jack Burgess had invited Joyce and I to join them at various Masonic Ladies Nights. These proved to be very enjoyable occasions and in due course after making enquiries I was duly initiated into the Loyal Berkshire Lodge of Hope no. 574 in Newbury. Here I was to meet other like-minded men, many of whom are still close friends today. I proceeded through the various offices and after ten years became Master of the Lodge. During this time I had also joined the Hungerford Chapter the Porchester Mark and Porchester Royal Ark Mariner Lodges and subsequently progressed "through the chair" of these Lodges.

To conclude, I hope that what I have written has given the reader a brief insight to what our village used to be and apologise if the later pages seem to deal with nothing other than myself.

However, each and every part of my life is tied in with the village and to the changes which have taken place there.

I am reminded of a piece of Masonic ritual an extract of which quotes 'that bond which forms an indissoluble attachment to that place whence you derived your birth and infant nurture'. In my younger days I did not imagine that my life would be filled with so many and varied activities and experiences and firmly believe that when the time comes for my ashes to be planted in the family plot in the local churchyard and our choir sing a few of the old favourites, that no one could wish to have spent a lifetime in a more pleasant village than Chieveley.

ISBN 142510246-8

9 781425 102463